LOVE HABITS

LOVE HABITS

Easy Strategies for a Stronger, Happier Relationship

Lori Ann Davis, MA

Illustrations by Sam Kalda

For general information on our other products and services or to obtain technical support, please contact our Customer Care Department within the United States at (866) 744-2665, or outside the United States at (510) 253-0500.

Rockridge Press publishes its books in a variety of electronic and print formats. Some content that appears in print may not be available in electronic books, and vice versa.

Interior and Cover Designer: Regina Stadnik
Art Producer: Hannah Dickerson
Editor: Meera Pal
Production Editor: Matthew Burnett

Illustrations © Sam Kalda, 2020.
Decorative pattern courtesy of iStock.
Author photograph courtesy of Donna Jernigan/Moments by Donna

ISBN: Print 978-1-64739-231-4 | eBook 978-1-64739-232-1

R0

I dedicate this book to the readers. With a little effort, your relationship can continue to grow and deepen over time. May the ideas in this book help you create a relationship that is better than you ever thought possible.

CONTENTS

INTRODUCTION

I have spent more than 35 years of my life in a happy, loving, long-term relationship. Has it always been easy to maintain this level of happiness? Definitely not. All relationships have their share of difficulties, and mine is no different. There were times when my partner and I were dealing with ups and downs outside the relationship and times when we were not as close as a couple. The one thing that has remained the same is my commitment to the relationship. I have a choice to make every day: I can let the small things bother me, or I can find the perfection in my partner and in our relationship, and be thankful for all he contributes to my life. My partner and I are different in many ways. We have different personalities and habits. We sometimes have different beliefs and viewpoints. These could cause tension and arguments in the relationship. Instead, I choose to accept and appreciate the differences between us and all he adds to my life without trying to change him.

I have spent my entire career working with couples, first as a marriage and family therapist and now as a relationship coach. My passion has always been to help people create and maintain loving relationships. I believe you can have a fabulous relationship if you know how. It doesn't have to be complicated, and small, simple acts practiced daily can make a big difference. The information I share in this book comes from my education, my years of working with clients, and my personal experience. I know firsthand that committed relationships are not always easy. When two unique individuals try to blend their lives, it does not happen without some challenges. I not only teach the habits discussed in the book, I practice them to build and maintain my loving relationship. I make a choice daily to choose love. With some effort, it works for my relationship, and I believe it can work for yours as well.

INTRODUCTION

This book was written for committed couples at various stages in their relationship, including the early stage of dating, engaged couples, and those in long-term relationships. You will find useful information as well as practical tips and exercises to guide and assist you in building and maintaining your relationship—no matter what stage you are in. No one teaches us how to have great relationships. My goal is to help you understand the natural cycle of relationships and how to navigate them successfully. We all start happy, and then conflicts arise. This is common. Love is not enough. Life gets complicated, but relationships do not have to when you have the right information and support. Couples can feel disconnected from time to time. This book provides you with easy-to-form habits that will allow you to create a deeper connection and stay connected no matter what else is going on in your life. You will also learn the importance of creating and maintaining emotional and physical intimacy in your relationship along with simple, easy-to-implement ideas for improving your connection.

We all long for closeness and emotional connection with our partner. Relationships are a team effort. They are shaped by choices you make, allowing you to grow and learn together, making each other a priority. I will be there to help you create strategies and love habits that guide you toward a stronger, happier, more intimate relationship.

—Lori Ann Davis

HOW TO USE THIS BOOK

I am excited for you to use this book to develop love habits that will help you build a stronger, more intimate relationship. You do not have to read the whole book from beginning to end. If you are a couple looking to address a specific relationship issue, jump right in to that specific chapter and start there. As you work through the book, you will notice that each chapter focuses on one specific habit. This allows you to work on one area of your relationship at a time and then move on when you are ready. You can also go back to specific chapters from time to time as needed.

I encourage you to work through all the chapters at some point. To strengthen your intimate relationship with your partner it's important to develop healthy habits in all areas. Even if you feel like your relationship is strong in a particular area, read the chapter and do the exercises anyway. You might be surprised by the positive impact it has.

This book is designed to help you understand the science and importance behind bonding and intimacy in a committed relationship. It is designed to provide habits to couples looking to strengthen their connection with their significant other. It is intended for use with your partner. To gain the most from the exercises I suggest doing them together. I understand, though, that sometimes, couples may be so disconnected that this is not possible. One person in the partnership may not initially be interested in this type of book or these types of exercises. If this is the case for you, that is okay. I encourage you to read the book and do the exercises yourself. Practice the love habits in each chapter, remembering that becoming the best partner you can be has the potential to change your relationship for the better. Making even small changes in your relationship can improve it, even if your partner isn't initially participating. So, go ahead and get started.

I suggest committing to one or two habits for a week or two. Practice one habit at a time and don't try to change your entire relationship all at once. There may be obstacles along the way as you learn new things. Be prepared for any conflict that might arise and use the techniques you are learning to deal with those. You can always step back and take smaller steps, if necessary. You might want to establish a reward you agree on for successfully creating and practicing each new habit. For example, plan a date night at the end of each chapter you successfully complete or a weekend getaway once you finish the book. Celebrate your achievements together! The ultimate goal is to adopt these habits to develop the kind of loving relationship you have always wanted.

SEEKING HELP

This book uses general terms that apply to most relationships, but not everyone will fit this generalization. Specifically, if you feel you are in a physically or emotionally abusive relationship, your first priority is to ensure your safety. Reach out to a local domestic violence agency or contact the National Domestic Violence Hotline for help by calling 1-800-799-7233 or online at TheHotline.org. If at any time you feel you are in immediate danger, call 911.

CHAPTER 1

RELATIONSHIP 101

Being part of a loving, supportive, intimate relationship is one of the best experiences life offers. There is nothing like that feeling of new love, with all the hormones that are released helping us feel attracted and connected to one another. In this chapter, we will dig into the biology of love, helping you understand the science behind why humans bond and what happens in your brain when you meet someone and fall in love.

Relationships go through stages, and the initial honeymoon stage eventually wears off. Couples begin to notice flaws in each other, differences of opinions arise, and partners can fall into routines that do not serve the best interest of the relationship. It isn't uncommon for couples to begin to drift apart at this stage, and love can begin to unravel.

There are key factors that contribute to a failing relationship, including poor communication, negative interactions, and unresolved conflict. We will look at each to help you know what signs to look for. Next, we will delve into the different types of intimacy—emotional, intellectual, experiential, and physical—helping you cultivate each to enhance your relationship.

There is no doubt that relationships take time and effort, but the results are worth it! There are so many reasons to work on creating a happier, more intimate bond with your partner. Being in a committed, loving relationship affects all areas of your life, including your mental and physical health, leading to a longer, happier life.

Anatomy of a Relationship

The first stage of a relationship is romantic love. It is that time when you first meet someone and can't stop thinking about them. You can't wait to see each other, you want to look your best, and your heart skips a beat when they call. The beginning of a relationship feels wonderfully exciting and fun. It is sometimes called the honeymoon phase and is when you find yourself "falling in love."

Eventually the phase begins to wear off. It is a natural progression and is something to be expected. Most couples assume they will continue to feel as good as they did in the beginning and are disappointed when they don't. They get frustrated and start to focus on the negatives in their relationship, assuming they have to settle for being unhappy. However, conflict and struggles are common in relationships. Couples can and do feel dissatisfied with each other from time to time. The important thing to remember is that you can learn how to move beyond dissatisfaction and build a relationship that is stronger and more satisfying than you thought possible.

SUMMER OF LOVE

Falling in love feels wonderful. You awaken thinking of that person, and thoughts of them fill your day with a sense of intense joy. You want to make them happy, and by doing so, your happiness increases. You start to daydream about a future together and find it hard to concentrate on other things. In the early stage of relationships, you see the best in the other person and find it hard to believe you could be so lucky to have met someone so perfect. It feels so good to know this special person is in love with you—and you love them in return! You want to spend all your time together, and your relationship is full of passion and excitement. You both put forth a lot of effort to show up as the best version of yourself, trying to make the best impression you can to keep the relationship going.

You focus on the things you have in common, while differences go unnoticed or are dismissed as not important. The idea of anything being wrong seems inconceivable.

FALL INTO LOVE

After a period, hormones settle, reality sets in, and most couples settle into a routine as the newness and excitement wear off. During this phase you might resort to repetitive kinds of date nights and become a little lazy in making the other person a priority, and passion can subside. You fall into predictable behaviors and do not look forward to spending time together as much as you used to. Couples simply stop putting in the extra effort and start to take each other for granted—without even realizing it. As you become more comfortable with each other, you start to let down your guard, showing parts of yourself you may have hidden in the beginning of the relationship.

You may start to notice habits or traits about your partner that you don't like. Problems or differences of opinion arise, and you have to work on problem solving together. The changes in the relationship can cause couples to focus more on the negatives, which can lead one or both to be discontented.

WINTER OF DISCONTENT

Inevitably, life gets in the way, and conflicts arise. Couples begin to lose their initial connection, and the feelings of joy and excitement they once had decline, along with the spark and passion. Disagreements and arguments begin to occur more regularly. Couples can begin to drift apart without even realizing it. Communication is essential to any healthy long-term relationship. As time goes on, couples typically do not communicate frequently or effectively, which may to lead to one or both partners feeling as though they have not been heard or understood by the other.

A common cause of growing discontent in relationships is unresolved conflict. Couples can get stuck in power struggles without knowing how to resolve them. In a successful relationship, both partners must take an active role in pleasing each other. When you stop taking initiative in love, both of you may start to take each other for granted, and the relationship can become stagnant. Making the other person a priority is essential.

Couples may also end up decreasing the amount of time they spend together when they get busy with life's demands. They stop connecting physically and emotionally, forgetting to let their partner know how much they care with words and actions. Having an understanding of this stage of a relationship and knowing how it can be handled can determine the couple's future happiness.

The Science of Human Bonding

Relationships can bring comfort, happiness, and unity. They can also cause grief, stress, and frustration. So, why do you work so hard to make someone else happy? Why do you endure stress and compromise? Simply put, you long to feel connected to another human being. Those connections affect how you feel about your work, your life, and yourself in general. Your overall happiness, your physical health, and even the length of your life are significantly influenced by the quality of your relationships. Individuals with strong emotional ties are better equipped to handle stressors that come up in day-to-day life. Humans have a fundamental desire to feel needed, loved, and cared for. We long to provide that for someone else as well, which is why we seek intimate relationships. Creating and maintaining an intimate relationship can be one of the most rewarding experiences of your life. The need to be close to another person begins in infancy and continues for the rest of your life.

Love is not just emotional but also biological. Social interactions trigger mental and physical processes in your brain that spread throughout your body. This is why you feel so good during the romantic love stage of a relationship. Biology is actually helping you fall in love—and stay in love.

A Harvard Medical School study titled "Love and the Brain" discusses the science of love. The study looks at the variety of hormones that play an important role in the biology of love. One such hormone is **oxytocin**, known as the *bonding hormone*. It facilitates behaviors such as eye contact and other social behaviors that create a feeling of being emotionally connected to the other person, which help create bonds between two people. Oxytocin is released when kissing and engaging in physical touch. **Vasopressin** is another hormone important in the biology of love. It is often called the *monogamy hormone* because it is responsible for creating intense loving memories during passionate times, causing you to want to repeat those experiences. **Endorphins** are also released into your body during times of physical touch or when you smile at a loved one or have positive thoughts about your partner. Endorphins are calming to your system and sometimes even act as painkillers.

BRAIN CHEMISTRY

While we may feel love in our hearts, the genesis is in our brains. The brain is flooded with a variety of hormones that carry a biological message throughout your body, helping you create and maintain lasting relationships. This rush of hormones causes the intense feelings of excitement and attraction we feel. Dopamine, known as the pleasure hormone, is produced by the hypothalamus and is released when we

do something that feels good. High levels
mine cause you to crave the attention of
partner. It is associated with motivation, reward, and goal-directed behaviors. This creates that sense of excitement, making the other person feel special and unique, leading us to envision a future together. Romantic love and attraction can activate the brain's opioid system, the part of the brain that causes us to be attracted to something. To keep the feelings of attachment going in long-term relationships, you need to keep your dopamine levels high. You can do this by sharing novel experiences, such as doing new things on date nights, traveling, or taking classes together.

The Unraveling of Love

With the aid of the many hormones flowing throughout the body, it is no wonder couples go into a new relationship thinking everything is perfect. There is an assumption that everything is going to be amazing—until you enter the next inevitable stage in any relationship: the conflict stage. This stage can come and go at different times; you don't experience it just once. How you handle this stage, though, can either make or break your relationship.

We will take a closer look at how you communicate during times of conflict, which negative interactions are the most harmful, and what happens when you are unable to resolve conflicts in your relationship. By becoming aware of the indicators, you can learn alternative ways of behaving that will improve your relationship instead of harming it.

POOR COMMUNICATION

Communication can be one of the most effective ways to create and keep a strong, healthy relationship. Talking is important to keep you aware of your partner's needs, work out problems, and negotiate and settle disagreements. If done correctly, communication is healthy and beneficial; however, there are times it can become harmful. How you communicate during conflict is an indicator of the overall success of the relationship.

Negative communication not only makes a relationship difficult but also can be the catalyst for the end of the partnership. In my experience, this is one of the top reasons relationships deteriorate and why couples seek counseling. Everyone needs to feel heard and understood; otherwise, we do not feel loved. Often, couples fall into a pattern of criticism and sarcasm. When you get in the habit of focusing on your partner's faults, this can set the tone for the rest of the conversation, causing your partner to either shut down or become defensive. The feelings brought up during a time of conflict don't just evaporate once the conflict is over. They can linger, permeating the relationship as a whole.

NEGATIVE INTERACTIONS

The research by John and Julie Gottman provides four primary indicators of a failing relationship. They have termed these four primary predictors the "Four Horsemen of the Apocalypse," and they include *criticism, contempt, defensiveness,* and *stonewalling.* All relationships can have some degree of each, but when they become a primary way of communicating, they are deadly to the relationship.

Criticism: When you criticize your partner, you focus on their flaws and pass judgment. Frequently, criticism starts with "you always" or "you never" language. Criticism erodes your partner's self-esteem and doesn't resolve problems.

Contempt: Contempt is probably the deadliest predictor. It is a way of asserting superiority over your partner to put them down, attacking their self-worth. Contempt can include harmful sarcasm, insensitive jokes, and eye-rolling.

Defensiveness: Defensiveness comes about when one partner feels attacked by the other or uses this type of communication to avoid taking responsibility for their own actions. They respond with an attack or complaint of their own to deflect the current issue. By not addressing relationship concerns, they avoid dealing with issues, causing frustration and burnout in the relationship.

Stonewalling: Stonewalling is a tactic by which one person removes themselves from all communication to avoid conflict. They might physically leave or refuse to communicate with their partner for a period. They might do this in an attempt to calm down when angry or as a way of showing disapproval, leaving their partner feeling frustrated and isolated.

In relationships, your positive interactions must outweigh the negative ones; otherwise, one or both partners will begin to avoid conversations and, ultimately, the relationship.

HEIGHTENED STATE OF ANXIETY

When conflict isn't resolved, couples can feel as though they are in a perpetual state of conflict, leading them to believe the problems being experienced can't be solved. They eventually lose the feeling of being in love. Conflict causes not only emotional stress but also physical reactions. The hormones adrenaline and cortisol are released, which can cause you to act impulsively. It becomes more difficult to have a constructive, healthy conversation, which then creates additional negative experiences. Couples begin to anticipate stressful interactions, causing their bodies to remain in a hyper-alert state. The memories of past conflict begin to influence the way they react to the current situation. They might become defensive or angry even before they hear what their partner has to say, or they might begin to avoid interactions altogether, expecting that they will be unpleasant. This can become a vicious cycle.

FIGHT OR FLIGHT

John walks in the door after a long day at work, looking forward to a quiet evening at home with his partner. As he goes to greet them, he sees that look of disgust on their face, and the rant begins about all the things John hasn't done and all the things he has done wrong. John knows from experience that this criticism will continue all evening. All John can think of is turning around and heading out the door or yelling back.

John is experiencing the fight-or-flight response, an internal process that prepares you for struggle or escape when you are in physical danger. This happens when you interpret a situation as threatening. Even though John isn't in physical danger, he is experiencing an innate reaction to stress. Hormones are released, giving him the added boost of energy to escape danger or stay and fight. But, in this case, there is no physical danger.

Staying physiologically on guard against danger, even when you just interpret the situation as stressful, has negative affects emotionally and physically. This gives you even more reason to learn to handle conflict with your partner in a more constructive way.

Happy Memories

All relationships have ups and downs, and some are more vivid in your memories than others. Remembering past experiences you have had as a couple can elicit those same feelings in the present. Emotional memories hold a great deal of power and can have a big impact on your relationship. If you are willing, take some time to think about your relationship with your partner.

- How did you first meet?
- What attracted you to the other person?
- Why did you decide to become a couple?
- How did you resolve your first fight?
- What are your favorite memories together?
- What else comes to mind?

Encourage your partner to do the same. You can have as much or as little structure as you wish to this exercise. Find a way to document each of your memories. This can be with a writing journal or a file on your computer.

- What kind of memories does this exercise trigger?
- Are there more happy ones or sad ones?

While experiencing challenging times in your relationship, it is often easier to remember negative interactions. When life isn't as challenging, it can be easier to remember positive memories. Focusing on negative memories contributes to feeling angrier or more guarded toward your partner in the present. Our feelings are influenced by the stories we tell, for better or worse. Positive memories elicit feelings of emotional connection and love. If you are trying to improve your relationship, it is time to shift your perspective—remembering good times is a great way to start.

The Four Types of Intimacy

When you think of intimacy, you probably think of some form of physical touch. However, truly connecting with another person involves different types of intimacy beyond physical touch. Creating a bond with another person requires a combination of four types of intimacy: emotional, intellectual, experiential, and physical.

As the initial romantic phase of a relationship begins to wear off, it becomes even more important to foster intimacy in all areas to maintain a thriving relationship. This does not mean you have to work on all areas at once but, rather, over the course of the relationship, strive to grow together as a couple in all areas.

Intimacy is a process that develops as you learn more about each other and grow together as a couple. You are always changing, and so is your relationship. There will be times when you connect more on one level than another, and you will probably be more comfortable in some areas of intimacy than others.

Exploring the different areas of intimacy provides a wonderful opportunity for you to grow and develop on a personal level. By exploring all four types of intimacy with your partner, you connect in a variety of ways, deepening your feelings for each other while furthering your enjoyment of time spent together. The more you learn and grow together, the less likely it is your relationship will become stagnant.

Developing intimacy takes communication, time, attention, and commitment to your partner and the relationship. Learning more about the different types of intimacy gives you new ways to relate and grow together. Although intimacy can't be forced, couples can and are encouraged to work on all four types to deepen their connection. Start where you are most comfortable, and then add something new a little at a time. This book provides the skills and ideas to help.

EMOTIONAL INTIMACY

Emotional intimacy is caring about the other person in the relationship and being interested in their feelings. It is the ability to share your innermost thoughts, knowing you are safe to express both happy times and struggles, feeling you will always be supported. Each person in the relationship feels able to express themselves and be vulnerable, knowing the other person will respond in a loving, supportive way. Your partner should be the one person with whom you know you can share anything. They are the first person you go to when something exciting happens or when something upsetting occurs. You don't hesitate to tell them what is on your mind because you feel safe and accepted.

Emotional intimacy is enhanced when you share your moments of doubt, fear, sadness, and pain with your partner. It's knowing that you can share embarrassing moments with your partner and that they will not only understand but also support you. You may even be able to laugh together about what happened while still feeling safe and loved. Emotional intimacy is being able to share your thoughts and beliefs knowing you will not be judged.

To build emotional intimacy both partners must be willing to take a risk and open up to each other to share what is on their minds and in their hearts on a deeper level. Conversations need to go beyond superficial day-to-day life events. You can build emotional intimacy by asking your partner questions; be curious and listen to their responses without judgment. The conversations should be constructive and include sharing a difficult subject. Your relationship should be your safe haven. It is the place you feel completely loved for who you are. Make it a priority to spend uninterrupted time together to learn more about your partner on a deeper level.

INTELLECTUAL INTIMACY

Intellectual intimacy is an exchange of thoughts, ideas, and opinions—a meeting of the minds. These are meaningful conversations where you share your thoughts about life, interests, dreams, and values. When was the last time you had an interesting and stimulating conversation with your partner? This might include talking about current events or sharing playful banter or sarcasm with each other. Maybe it is a conversation about a book you read, a movie you saw, or a new hobby you want to explore together. Next time you sit down to dinner, ask your partner questions about something you know they are interested in. Allow them to share their knowledge with you. Brainstorm about a new hobby you could share. Have fun learning something new as a couple. Play a game together one evening, enjoying some fun competition.

For each couple, intellectual intimacy will be different depending on your personalities and interests. For some it will be deeply intellectual, and for others it will be lighter and more fun-loving. These interactions should be satisfying and challenging at the same time, sharing similarities and differences of opinion. They build and support the couple's friendship, increasing and maintaining their bond through an intellectual connection. Once you get into the habit, connecting intellectually will be something you look forward to.

EXPERIENTIAL INTIMACY

Experiential intimacy occurs when a couple spends time together sharing an activity without other distractions, allowing them to focus their attention on each other. This is a way of communicating to your partner that they are important to you while relaxing and enjoying each other's company. It gives you something to look forward to. Your life can get busy; if you don't make time together a priority, you run the risk of putting off connecting this way.

Suggestions for experiential intimacy include:

- Date nights
- Going for walks together
- Sharing a hobby

What does your partner like to do for fun? Ask them to let you join them. Work together on a project around the house, changing it from a chore to a bonding experience. Try a new activity together or a new cuisine on your next date night. Get out of your normal routine. Make a list of possibilities and add a few to your calendar.

Take time to share small things on a regular basis and to try new things together. These common experiences give you something to talk and laugh about, and memories to share in the future. It isn't what you do but the experience of doing it together that brings you closer, providing an environment for feelings of love and romance to grow.

PHYSICAL INTIMACY

Physical intimacy means being affectionate with each other in a variety of ways, not just sexually. It can include hugging, kissing, holding hands, massaging, cuddling, and other forms of physical touch. Physical touch bonds two people, creating a closeness you only share with each other and building a deep emotional connection.

So often couples avoid physical touch because, at the end of the day, they are tired and this seems like one more thing to do. In reality, once you get started, the energy follows. Physical intimacy releases hormones, including oxytocin, helping you recreate those feelings of closeness you had at the beginning of the relationship. The hormones released will motivate you to desire physical touch and allow you to enjoy the experience. When we talk about physical intimacy, couples often only think about sexual touch and don't realize the benefits of lingering kisses, longer hugs, cuddling time on the couch, or simply being physically playful with each other. The more touch you add to your relationship, the better you will feel about your partner and your relationship.

When you engage in physical intimacy, you focus on the positive attributes of your partner and are generally more tolerant, less critical, and happier with each other. It creates a bond that has a positive effect on every aspect of your relationship, creating a higher rate of overall satisfaction.

Physical intimacy involves a degree of vulnerability and trust. Although emotional intimacy allows us to feel safe opening up to our partner, physical intimacy bonds us to our partner, increasing the emotional attachment we feel. What can you do as a couple to enhance your feelings of trust, enabling you to be more vulnerable with your needs and feeling confident your partner will meet them?

The Benefits of Working on Your Relationship

All relationships have ups and downs, and it is not unusual to have times when you feel close to each other and times when you drift apart. It takes intentional effort to keep the connection strong in relationships. Couples can grow apart without even realizing it. They can end up feeling disconnected from each other. This may stem from external circumstances, like an illness or job stress, or from internal stress, such as an argument or differences of opinion that do not get resolved. Couples can, either intentionally or unintentionally, begin to pull away from each other and start leading separate lives.

When couples feel emotionally and physically disconnected from each other, they can begin to feel very alone in the relationship. They might even question their commitment to each other. When your relationship isn't going well, it permeates all aspects of your life, including job performance, sleep, overall health, and even self-esteem. Although down times may be normal, it is important to address them.

The benefits of being in a happy relationship go beyond the relationship itself. People who work on their relationships are happier in general, even within the ups and downs. The relationship doesn't have to be perfect, as long as there is an overall feeling that you can count on your partner. Working toward a happier, more intimate relationship is beneficial in so many ways. A happy, satisfying relationship can help you live longer while also enjoying improved overall mental and physical health.

IMPROVED MENTAL HEALTH

Humans are, by nature, social creatures. We have an innate desire to be in relationships. Maintaining meaningful relationships provides companionship, support, self-esteem, and intimacy. Individuals in loving relationships are less likely to be depressed, as they are, generally, more content and satisfied with their lives. Relationships provide a buffer from the outside world, giving you a place to feel safe and loved.

Working together on goals and making plans for the future, even just the weekend, keep you mentally stimulated and give you something to look forward to. Keeping relationships strong and healthy takes commitment and effort, but the results are definitely worth it. Couples who have strong loving relationships have a better overall outlook on life. They feel more secure and at ease and enjoy an increased overall feeling of joy in all areas of their lives. The benefits of a healthy relationship make you a healthier, happier person.

IMPROVED PHYSICAL HEALTH

Strongly connected relationships are not only good for your mental outlook; they also benefit your physical health. Do you know your relationship can even improve your immune system?

According to Dr. Robert Waldinger's research, positive, supportive relationships decrease stress levels, helping you feel more relaxed. Being more relaxed has a positive effect not only on your immune system but also on your overall health. Caring about another person releases stress-reducing hormones, which can help lower blood pressure and are good for overall heart health. A 2017 study in *Psychoneuroendocrinology* found that married individuals had lower levels of the stress hormone cortisol than those who were never married or were previously married. Happy couples also experience a better quality of sleep, according to a 2015 study in the journal *Sleep*. Levels of oxytocin, also known as the *cuddle hormone,* rise when you physically interact with your partner. When you spend time in bed together cuddling or being intimate, you feel calm and protected. This helps you fall asleep more easily, resulting in a more restful night.

Being in a relationship can also motivate you to take better care of yourself by eating better and exercising more to stay healthy and look good for your partner. It is easier to stick to a healthy eating plan and exercise routine when you are not doing it alone. Couples typically encourage each other to monitor personal health and seek treatment, when necessary. A happy relationship is overall good medicine.

A LONGER LIFE

Being in a committed, happy, loving relationship can add years to your life, which can be attributed to reduced stress, better sleep, and healthier habits. Couples overall tend to take better care of themselves, drinking and smoking less, eating healthier, and exercising more. It is easier to adopt healthier lifestyle habits when you have someone to support you. Couples are more likely to have a strong desire to stay healthy and active so they can enjoy life together, in both the present and the future.

People in caring relationships are less likely to feel isolated, lonely, and depressed, especially as they get older, all leading to better health and longevity. Having a partner present to offer encouraging words, to hold motivating conversations with, or to offer a shoulder to cry on helps you feel stronger, happier, and more confident. Mental health is related to physical health, so having someone there for companionship is important. The support and encouragement couples provide each other reduce stress and provide an environment for positive mental and emotional health, all of which contributes to a longer, healthier life.

CHAPTER 2

CREATE A COMMON VISION

Relationships typically begin with great excitement, but over time, that newness wears off, and they can become routine and stagnant. How do you prevent that from happening? Creating a common vision is a great way to enhance your relationship, strengthening your bond to create the relationship you desire. When you intentionally craft a relationship vision with your partner, you feel as if you are working together toward a common goal. Instead of living your life and hoping your relationship moves in the direction you desire, you are proactive in setting a course and steering your relationship in the right direction. You discover commonalities and differences that can be addressed and negotiated toward the common goal. This chapter teaches you how to create a relationship vision and how to make implementing the vision a habit you can both look forward to.

Common Goals and Dreams

Conversations within a relationship can become superficial, focusing on day-to-day tasks instead of being of greater depth as they were in the beginning of the relationship. This shift often happens without either partner realizing it. Life gets in the way, and the relationship takes a back seat. Couples start to function on automatic pilot. Most of us are not taught how to maintain loving relationships. Some people think the absence of problems means a relationship is good. However, so much more is possible when a couple knows how to create and keep a deeper bond—through the good times and the bad.

Good communication and a common vision help a couple develop emotional intimacy (see page 13), which is a key component in a stronger connection. If you do not know what your dreams are, it is hard to work together to create a life you are both happy with. Unless you and your partner share the same relationship vision, you are bound to run into trouble. Yet most couples don't know how to create a vision with conscious intent. Sharing your thoughts, dreams, feelings, desires, and needs creates an opportunity for a deeper connection and a plan for your future. A shared vision pulls together individual dreams, values, and needs.

Build a Habit

I encourage you to schedule a weekly time to sit down with your partner and discuss your relationship and your life together as a couple. Make this something you look forward to. It could be part of date night, an evening walk, or something you do over Saturday morning breakfast. Create a routine so it becomes part of your life together, becoming a habit that keeps your relationship a priority. When you take time to review your relationship on a regular basis, it is much easier to make small adjustments as needed rather than attempting to resolve bigger issues that build over time. Regularly discussing your vision also allows you to make necessary adjustments as your dreams or situations change. This can help you stay connected and work like a team supporting each other. So, how do you do this?

DEFINE CORE VALUES

The first step is to determine your personal core values for the relationship. Core values are the fundamental beliefs of a person or relationship. They are the guiding principles that dictate your personal behavior. Many times, relationships are formed based on shared core values. Some common core values for a relationship include *honesty, reliability, open communication, ambition, kindness,* and *family.*

Make a list, thinking about what is truly important to you. Ask your partner to do the same. You can't work together as a couple if you don't know what is important to each other. Explore each other's values, ask questions, and be curious.

RELATIONSHIP VISION

Now that you know each other's personal core values, it is time to delve into your personal vision for the relationship. Creating a relationship vision is a conscious way of exploring what you truly want and need from your relationship. It provides a direction and concrete goals. It helps provide clarity as to what is important to you in the relationship, guiding you in the decisions you make as a couple. If you are unsure what to include in your vision, take some time to imagine your life with your partner. What is important to you in order to be happy? Vision statements are written in the present tense, using positive language. Be as specific as you can. Remember, you can always change your vision as your relationship and life progress. Some areas to explore are finances, communication, conflict resolution, emotional intimacy, sexuality, family time, and career.

An example of a relationship vision may be something such as *"We easily talk about disagreements and resolve problems respectfully."* At the end of this chapter, you will have an opportunity to work on your own relationship vision.

SHARE VISION STATEMENTS

You will create a relationship vision, one specific and meaningful to you. It is equally important to share that vision with your partner to gain a better understanding of each other. When you come together with understanding and clarity, you can resolve any feelings of uncertainty and frustration. Often, couples think they are on the same page and know what is important to their partner only to find later that they are mistaken.

After creating your personal vision, it is important to come together and create a shared vision that incorporates ideas from both partners. Creating shared visions helps you become a team with common goals. You are no longer wandering aimlessly but acting with a purpose. You will find areas of agreement and areas of divergence requiring discussion. Bringing these areas to the surface means you can consciously come together to create a shared dream. This dream will guide the decisions you make as a couple and help you stay connected.

RELATIONSHIP ROAD MAP

Once you develop your shared relationship vision, it is important to create action steps to get there. This is like creating a road map with directions for how you will get to your destination. It also creates clear relationship goals you can track, states who is responsible for what actions, and sets a timeline for accomplishing them.

It can be helpful to prioritize your goals. Which are immediate, and which are longer term? You might have ongoing plans for regular date nights and a more long-term goal of buying a home. Each goal will have action steps to help you stay on task and accomplish the goal. You can always go back and make necessary adjustments as required. This is not something you do once but is part of your relationship growth and development. You should make a point of discussing your goals on a regular basis, looking at what works and considering what (if anything) needs to be changed. The more attention you focus on your relationship, the greater chance you have of creating the relationship you really want.

Create a Vision

You and your partner will each need a pen and something to write on. Set aside about 1 hour to work on this exercise.

1. Begin with each of you individually writing a list of goals you have for the relationship and your future. Be sure to cover all areas discussed in the chapter and add others that are important to you.
2. Describe the relationship you desire to create in the present tense, using a positive tone.
3. Come together and compare your lists.
4. Take time to discuss each goal in detail.
5. Use your individual ideas to create a list you develop together. Your goal is to combine your individual visions into a relationship vision.
6. Review the list and identify the top priorities.
7. Create a habit for reviewing the list and deciding on action steps to take.

8. Use your weekly time together to talk about anything that needs immediate attention and then review your vision.
    - How are you doing in each area?
    - Are there one or two areas that need attention?
9. Make a plan for the week. Doing so helps you stay focused on creating the relationship you desire.
10. What concrete actions can you take to work toward your goals?

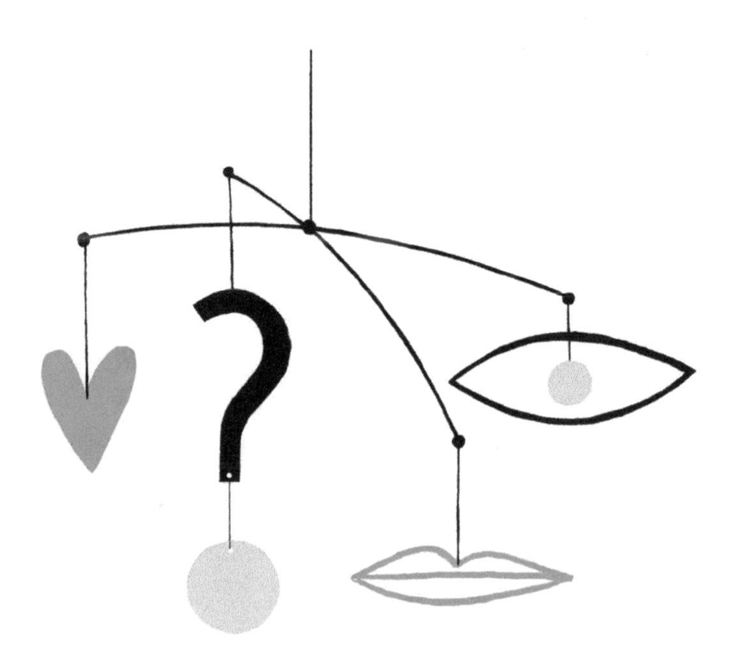

CHAPTER 3

BE CURIOUS ABOUT ONE ANOTHER

It's important to feel as though you are a priority in your partner's life. Giving your undivided attention is an amazing way of showing your love. Being curious about your partner's thoughts, feelings, experiences, and dreams shows that you are engaged. We all want to feel accepted and understood by our partner—the most important person in our lives. How do you make this a regular part of your relationship? It starts with being present and giving your partner your undivided attention. Connect with your partner on a regular basis. Ask questions that allow them to share on a deeper level to foster intimacy. Set aside time to do this in a consistent way, and before long, you will look forward to these conversations. At the end of this chapter is a fun exercise to do together to get you started.

Be Curious

We pursue our partner in the beginning of the relationship and spend lots of time and effort getting to know them. We ask lots of questions to learn as much as we can about this new person in our life. We can spend hours talking and listening to each other's stories, learning about each other one layer at a time. As the relationship progresses, we ask deeper and more meaningful questions. We move from asking about jobs and hobbies to values, dreams, and influential experiences. As time goes on, we assume we know all there is to know about each other. Our conversations become superficial instead of the kind that draw you closer and create profound connections. Being in a strong, healthy relationship that stands the test of time requires a couple to remain curious about each other. We continue to grow and change throughout our lives, which means there is always something to talk about. Being curious encourages your partner to open up and share, causing them to feel more connected in the relationship. When you take time to share with each other on a deep level, you feel accepted and understood, which increases your emotional intimacy (see page 13) and creates a stronger relationship.

Build a Habit

Just like anything else, if you don't make a conscious effort to do things differently, you fall back into the same routines. You can fall into a habit of making assumptions and judging the other person, causing discord in your relationship. Instead, foster a habit of curiosity, which takes intention and practice until it becomes second nature. Being present for your partner, to listen and learn more about them, helps you make choices that foster intimacy and connection. When you take time to ask questions and listen to the answers, you avoid disagreements and create deeper connections.

BE PRESENT

Start by being present and giving your partner your full attention. Be careful not to take them for granted. This means being emotionally present, not just physically present. Set aside daily time to find out about their day. Talk about issues that need to be dealt with. Relax and enjoy each other's company. When you connect, make eye contact and be present. That means staying off your phone and refraining from any other activity. Make time for your partner to show you care and let them know how important they are to you.

MAKE BETTER CHOICES

You have the opportunity every day to make choices about how you think and act toward your partner. These choices have a major impact on your relationship, and being conscious of these choices will help you create habits that can make a big difference in how happy and satisfied you are with your partner.

Repeated choices become habits. These choices and habits have a great deal of power in your life. Small things done regularly make a big difference in your relationship. When you make the relationship a priority by connecting on a daily basis, your partner will feel loved, accepted, safe, and cherished. Instead of assuming you know how your partner feels or what their thoughts are about something, take time to find out. Be curious about your partner's needs. Needs change over time as life changes, so make the effort to discover what your partner needs from you in the relationship—it's one of the best ways to avoid conflict in a relationship.

ASK QUESTIONS

Take time to ask about things that are important to your partner. Show an active interest in their life. Posing open-ended questions invites conversation rather than a short "yes" or "no" response. For instance, instead of asking your partner if they had a good day, ask, *"What was the most interesting thing that happened at work today?"* Be curious about your partner's dreams and goals. They change, so checking in gives you a chance to provide ongoing support. You are trying to tap into your partner's experience of the world instead of assuming you know what it is.

SET ASIDE TIME

Life will always get in the way if you do not make time for what is important in yours. Try to create a ritual for connecting. Maybe you spend time each morning asking your partner about their upcoming day. Is there anything unusual happening? Is there anything they need your help with? I love connecting with my husband at the end of the day. We take time to check in with each other every evening. It is a connection ritual we started when dating, and we continue it to this day. The goal is to make this a habit—so why not put it on your calendar? If you are not having a regular date night, it might be time to start. This is a great time to give one another your undivided attention, allowing each partner to share thoughts, feelings, needs, dreams, desires, even fantasies. Consider trying something new periodically, like a new activity, a new restaurant, or anything to expand your horizons. It will give you even more to talk about.

Discovery Game

I encourage you to play the following discovery game with your partner. Feel free to add more questions. You and your partner should each answer the questions. I suggest writing down the answers. Once you have both finished, review each of your answers together to see how well you know each another.

- What is your partner's favorite style of music?
- Who was your partner's closest childhood friend?
- What does your partner feel most insecure about?
- Where was your partner born?
- What was your partner wearing when you first met?
- What is your partner's favorite movie?
- What was your partner like as a child?
- What was your partner's favorite job?
- What is your partner's most irrational fear?
- In what setting is your partner happiest?
- What country would your partner most like to visit?
- What is your partner's favorite thing to spend money on?

- If your partner could retire tomorrow, what would they do?
- What is your partner's favorite food?
- Whom does your partner consider the most influential person in their life?
- What is your partner's favorite way to relax?
- If your partner could meet one famous person, who would it be?
- If your partner could go back in time, what age would they like to relive?
- What is the one thing that irritates your partner most?
- What era in time would your partner like to visit?

love you

CHAPTER 4

BE THOUGHTFUL

Are you doing things daily to enhance your relationship? This chapter will help you develop small, easy-to-follow steps for things you can do on a regular basis to show your partner you care. This will help strengthen your relationship by building meaningful connections while making them a priority. Random acts of kindness that aren't so random are powerful ways to exhibit your devotion.

Be Thoughtful

Have you developed a habit of taking your partner for granted? We get busy in life, and our relationships can take a back seat. Life will always get in the way of building a meaningful connection if you let it. It is important to feel like you are part of a team. The little things are really what matter—they mean the most to us and bring us happiness. Grand gestures are nice, but random acts of kindness performed regularly are the most important. They are essential to the happiness of a relationship. It doesn't have to be difficult to create habits that will support and deepen your relationship. Small steps taken daily will become habits that will nurture your bond. Habits of love, appreciation, and gratitude are just as easy to foster as habits of criticism and resentment.

The best way to build a habit is to do something small but thoughtful every day. This reminds you both why you matter to each other. When you choose thoughts of love or to remember what you like about your partner, feelings of connection and love follow. What can you do every day to build your relationship?

SAY "THANK YOU"

Compliment and praise your partner. Be appreciative and say, "Thank you," for the things they do for you. Do this when you are talking to them or leave a note where they can find it. Do it in front of others as well. Show your partner you are proud of them. Try to keep this timely by recognizing things they do on a regular basis. I tell my husband "thank you" almost every day for unloading the dishwasher. I am truly appreciative that he is doing something to make my morning easier. By acknowledging his effort, I make him feel appreciated. When you pay attention to the little things your partner does, you will appreciate your partner even more. And when you share that appreciation with your partner, they feel happier with you and the relationship.

HAVE FUN

Sometimes we take life too seriously. What can you do to add more fun to your relationship? It can be as simple as finding something to laugh about together, dancing in the living room, watching a funny movie, or anything light and playful. Life and relationships can become bogged down with heaviness from day-to-day problems. Taking a break, having fun, and laughing together are essential gifts you can give your partner for the welfare of your relationship. Laughing together lifts your spirits, reduces tension, and brings you closer together.

SURPRISE THEM

For no reason at all other than that you love and appreciate your partner, do something nice for them as a surprise. It can be something small and inexpensive—it isn't the item or gift but the thought that counts. Bring home a movie they like, make their favorite dinner, or take them out to do something they enjoy. Or complete a chore for them. For example, fill up their car with gas and run it through the car wash. It is all about the thought behind the gesture that says, *"I took time to think of something you would like and am giving it to you because you are important to me."*

LOVE SPEAK

Use words to tell your partner you are thinking about them and they are important to you. This can be something you do verbally, such as telling your partner how nice they look in the morning before heading off to work. It can be something you do in writing, such as leaving a note where they can find it telling them how much you love them or sharing a positive memory about your relationship. Send a random loving, flirty, or playful text or meme to your partner saying how much you love them, how much they mean to you, that you are thinking of them, or that you would choose them as your partner all over again. This is a great way to connect, and I recommend doing it daily.

Loving Behavior

Make a list of as many things you can think of that you like and appreciate about your partner. Think back to the past week, the past month, the past year. Focus on things they have done and qualities they possess that make you happy to have them as your partner.

Review the list often and add to it. The more you focus on the positives, the more positives you will notice. You can also think about why you chose your partner in the first place. Make sure those qualities are on your list.

Now, make a list of things you know your partner likes—those small random acts of kindness you can perform for them. If you are not sure, ask for their input. Ask what you could do to make their life easier. Be creative with your list.

Keep the lists handy and do something daily that lets them know you are thinking of them, you appreciate them, and you care.

Watch how your relationship begins to change for the better. You can share this exercise with your partner, or you can begin to practice it and watch them start to do things for you in return.

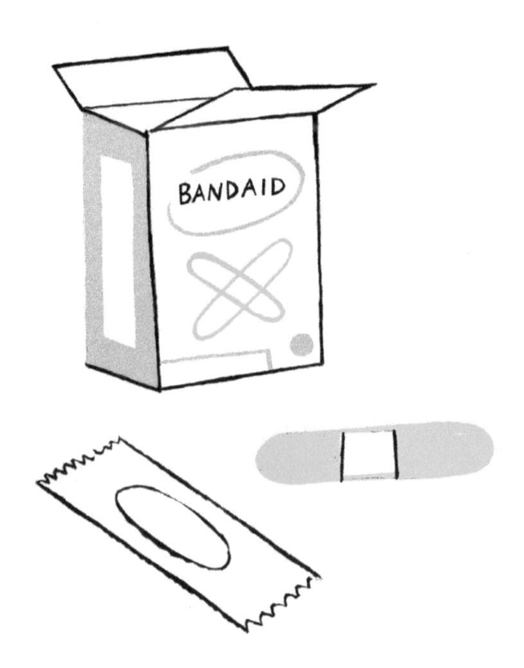
BANDAID

CHAPTER 5

APOLOGIZE

From time to time in a relationship, you may do something that hurts or offends your partner—whether you mean to or not. You are human and are not perfect. When you hurt your partner in some way, accept responsibility for your actions, acknowledge your mistake, and apologize. It is a way to be accountable, acknowledge their feelings, and let them know you will make every effort to act in a better way in the future.

This sounds simple, but apologizing can be difficult to do. To say you are sorry, you have to take responsibility for your actions, which can be uncomfortable and bring up all sorts of feelings you might not want to deal with. In this chapter we look at why it is important to apologize and how to do it in a way that is beneficial to everyone.

Say "Sorry"

When you think of apologizing, it can bring up a wide range of feelings. You might have been forced to apologize to others as a child. This might have made you feel bitter, ashamed, or even angry if you didn't think you did anything wrong. It makes some feel inadequate or as though the whole conflict is their fault. You might have been taught to apologize without really understanding the important role it plays in relationships or even how to offer a sincere apology.

Conflict is bound to arise in relationships from time to time. During times of conflict, you might act in ways that are not beneficial to the relationship. It happens to everyone. Learning to take full responsibility for your actions and acknowledging the impact your words and actions have and the hurt they cause are essential to moving beyond the conflict. These are times when an apology is owed; when done appropriately, it helps put the conflict behind you so you can move on.

Saying you are sorry and asking for forgiveness make up one of the most important factors of relationship satisfaction. Doing so takes effort, but it is worth it. Apologizing means you have to look at your actions, why you did what you did, and how you feel about your partner. For many people this is not a comfortable thing to do. It requires vulnerability and honesty with yourself and your partner. Pride can get in the way. A well-thought-out, appropriately sincere apology will help resolve issues and restore positive feelings between you and your partner, increasing your emotional connection.

Build a Habit

When you apologize, it is important to include some key elements. Apologies become easier when you know what to say. Here are some easy steps to help you learn how to apologize effectively. Once you learn how to apologize and experience the benefits of doing so, it will become something you will want to do when appropriate.

YOUR FEELINGS

Start with paying attention to how you feel when you do something wrong. Remember, it can be difficult to apologize when it really matters. Apologizing requires humility. You have to admit you have done something wrong—either purposefully or unintentionally. It can be hard on your self-esteem and your ego to admit wrongdoing, bringing up feelings of guilt or shame. Admitting you have something to apologize for isn't always easy to do. You are coming from a vulnerable place and might wonder how the apology will be received. You might have tried to apologize in the past but the other person did not accept your apology, or they might have even become angrier with you. Knowing that uncomfortable feelings might come up and being willing to move past them form the first step in learning how to apologize for the sake of your relationship.

YOUR PARTNER'S FEELINGS

When it is time to apologize, pay attention to your partner's feelings. Step outside your feelings and pay attention to how your partner feels about what is going on. How are they experiencing your words or actions? Taking time to tap into their experience and allowing them to share their feelings show you care. Doing so allows you to see your actions through their eyes, making a sincere apology easier.

REFLECT

Once you have a clear understanding of how your partner feels, it is easier to step out of the ego and reflect on your words or actions. You might not have meant to be hurtful, or maybe you were upset and, at the time, did mean it. But with reflection and understanding of the results, you can feel differently. Typically, when you step back and take time to process, hurting your partner is not the choice you would make. Empathy can be used to acknowledge and accept your behavior and connect with your partner on a deeper level. This is a great way to build trust in your relationship and learn from your behavior.

ACTION

When you focus on what is truly important—your relationship—apologizing becomes easier. Don't wait too long. The more time that passes, the more feelings of hurt, anger, or even resentment build. The longer you wait, the more the offense can grow in magnitude in the other person's mind, and the deeper the hurt becomes. This all makes it harder for you to apologize and less likely your apology will be accepted. The overall message you want to send is that your partner is a priority.

Apology Script

A sincere apology has a few key elements. The following is an example of how to apologize effectively and sincerely.

1. **Apologize in person whenever possible.** Sit down in person with your partner so you can make eye contact when you apologize.
2. **Let your partner know you made a mistake** and that your primary concern is your relationship. Be specific about what you did wrong.
3. **Tell your partner you are sorry.** You might say, *"I am sorry I was so late for our special dinner. I was inconsiderate and didn't appreciate all your effort."*
4. **Ask for forgiveness** and about what you can do to make it right, and listen to the response. *"Will you please forgive me? Our relationship is important to me. What can I do to make it up to you?"*

5. **Promise to do better moving forward.** Discuss how you can learn and grow from this experience to lessen the chance of it happening again. *"In the future, I will set a reminder on my phone to leave work in time so I won't be late."*

CHAPTER 6

BE VULNERABLE

A healthy relationship is one based on honesty, respect, and trust, where you feel safe being open and vulnerable. That said, many people have no idea how to create a space for both partners to feel safe being open and vulnerable. Vulnerability requires that you trust yourself and your partner to express yourself openly and without judgment. Vulnerability creates an environment for growth, deepening your love for each other. In this chapter you will learn about emotional intelligence, including the role it plays in relationships and how to increase yours. I provide ideas to guide you on your journey toward opening up with each other, thus increasing your trust and emotional intimacy with one another.

Building a Safe Space

Your relationship is your safe haven. It is the place you feel completely loved for who you are. Yet many people don't know what it means to create a safe space for each other. Bringing two people together from varying backgrounds, with different personalities, to form a relationship can include challenges. Some people are blessed with positive role models like parents or family members, but many are not. Both people in the relationship must be committed to creating a safe and vulnerable space to form the emotional intimacy a relationship needs to thrive.

It can be scary to open yourself up to someone else. Some people view this as a sign of weakness or are afraid of not being accepted. Being vulnerable with your partner requires that you accept yourself first before you can open up and share with someone else. Vulnerability builds trust, knowing your partner has your best interests at heart. Being with someone who holds you accountable and encourages you invites growth. Vulnerability encourages you to take responsibility for your feelings and builds confidence to share those feelings without judgment. It creates a strong bond between you and your partner, deepening your love and commitment and knowing this is the one person with whom you can truly be yourself and still be accepted and loved.

EMOTIONAL INTELLIGENCE

Developing emotional intelligence is important to having a strong, successful connection. But what does it mean to have emotional intelligence? The *Oxford English Dictionary* defines emotional intelligence as "the capacity to be aware of, control, and express one's emotions, and to handle interpersonal relationships judiciously and empathetically." Emotional intelligence allows you to interact with other people successfully. When you understand your own feelings, you can understand others. Emotional intelligence starts with learning to become aware of your feelings and emotions and, ultimately, those of others.

Day-to-day life can trigger a variety of emotions. Understanding why these emotions arise means you can, ultimately, control how you react to them, taking responsibility for *your* emotions and behavior. To do this, you must understand what triggers certain emotions within you and within others. For example, if someone yells at you, they might not even be angry with you. They might be feeling stress in another area of life, which comes out in a manner that appears directed at you. Realization of this allows you not to take it personally and ensures that you do not react in anger. You can learn to interpret situations and learn to understand other people's emotions and reactions.

Once you understand yourself better, it is easier to understand others and develop empathy for them. Emotional intelligence can strengthen your relationship, increase intimacy, and grow love. It is a lifelong process to continue to learn, improve, and refine.

IDENTIFY EMOTIONS

Start by noticing how you feel and label those feelings. There are so many more feelings than happy, sad, and angry. You might be frustrated, disappointed, or worried, to name a few. I suggest stopping during the day to notice how you feel. Get used to tapping into your emotions and naming them. Don't just say, *"I am upset."* Dig deeper to discover whether there is another feeling below "upset." Maybe you feel hurt. By better understanding what you feel, you can move to the next step in developing emotional intelligence.

UNLEARN EMOTIONAL BAD HABITS

Take time to consider how your emotions affect your thoughts and actions. You can't control your initial reaction to a situation, but you can learn to control the thoughts that follow, which will ultimately determine the decisions you make. Most people have an immediate reaction to situations based on beliefs learned early in life. Such beliefs may or may not serve your present best interests. We often react to situations based on these outdated beliefs, later regretting our words or actions. This happens when we overreact to a situation or react without learning what the other person intended. Your reaction may not have much to do with the event. It may have more to do with what your mind tells you the event means, causing beliefs to be triggered. It is beneficial to identify the patterns to learn appropriate ways of responding and communicating.

PRACTICE MINDFULNESS

The best way to practice mindfulness is to pause when you experience strong emotions and give yourself time to process the feelings before acting on them. Stop and observe your thoughts behind the feelings. What are you telling yourself about the interaction? Are you sure your interpretation is accurate, or would it be beneficial to ask for clarification? There are numerous ways to look at a situation. Even if the other person said or did something that warrants your strong reaction, there is merit in taking time to process your feelings. Once you are calmer, you can have a more productive conversation with the other person.

ASK TO BE HELD ACCOUNTABLE

Learning to break old patterns and deal with emotions more positively takes time and practice. It is a process of retraining your brain to react in a new way. The more you practice, the easier it gets. You are developing a new habit of intentionally checking your emotions, thoughts, and actions, striving for clarity and empathy in your interactions with others. It is beneficial to talk to your partner and let them know what you are doing. Ask them to help hold you accountable. They might notice your reactions before you do and can kindly and gently remind you to take a deep breath before reacting. They can proactively give you time and space to process things, making an agreement to talk about the situation later. Doing this for each other is a wonderful way to create a safe space.

Vulnerability Quiz

How vulnerable do you feel with your partner?

The following quiz is a great way to learn where you and your partner currently connect and where you have opportunities for a deeper connection. Take the quiz independently, and then share the results with one another. Talk about areas in which you can improve and about how much you enjoy the connections verified.

Answer each question with **Very True, Mostly True, Somewhat True,** or **Rarely True.** Use a notebook to record your answers.

1. My partner is emotionally available to me.
2. I feel comfortable sharing my insecurities with my partner.
3. I feel comfortable crying in front of my partner.
4. There is no topic that is off-limits with my partner.
5. I feel comfortable sharing embarrassing moments with my partner.
6. My partner is there to support me during stressful times.

7. I feel comfortable talking about sex and sexual needs with my partner.
8. My partner and I easily share goals and dreams about the future.
9. I feel heard and understood by my partner when there is a disagreement.
10. I feel like my partner loves me for who I am, just the way I am.

Build a Habit

Learning to be more vulnerable with your partner takes practice. The more you open up, the easier it becomes as you build a level of trust with each other. Vulnerability takes courage. Take small steps to move forward. It might seem scary at first, but the results are worth it. The best way to do this is to make it a priority in your relationship. Set aside time to connect on a daily basis. Start by sharing small things with your partner that are more comfortable and then ease into deeper topics. You can encourage each other in this new habit by giving your partner your full attention when they share with you. Validate their emotions and let them know you hear and understand them. Ask follow-up questions to learn more, encouraging communication. Be careful about rushing in to solve your partner's problems, though. Sometimes, all we really want is the other person to listen to us. If you feel as though it is appropriate to offer advice, ask your partner if it would be helpful. The most important thing is for them to feel heard and emotionally supported.

When we share experiences and feelings with one another in an authentic way, we feel closer to each other. Try it and see what happens in your relationship.

Open Up

Set aside a time when you know you can give your partner your undivided attention. Pick a topic about which you feel comfortable sharing.

- » A failure or mistake you've made
- » A fear or phobia
- » A lie you have told
- » A regret you hold on to
- » A dream you haven't shared
- » A pivotal moment in your life
- » Your biggest career goals
- » The scariest thing you have ever done
- » A fantasy you haven't shared
- » An experience you wish you could relive
- » Your greatest accomplishment
- » Something you would change if you had the chance
- » Your biggest guilty pleasure
- » Something you feel insecure about
- » The biggest risk you have ever taken
- » Your worst habit
- » Your most embarrassing moment

Discuss why you chose the topic, why it matters to you, and how it affects you. Have your partner reciprocate. Be vulnerable.

CHAPTER 7

TOUCH OFTEN

All humans need physical touch. Partners in a strong and connected relationship often participate in various forms of physical connection, which is essential to the success of any intimate relationship. In this chapter you will learn more about why physical touch is so important, along with ideas to add physical touch to your relationship. When we talk about physical touch, we are not exclusively talking about sex. People touch in many ways, and no one way is better than another. Join me in exploring ideas for adding more touch to your daily routine, helping you create a happier, more intimate relationship.

Be Affectionate

In the beginning of a relationship, there is usually a great deal of physical touch. As the relationship goes on, touch tends to decrease. As a relationship progresses, it is important to maintain physical intimacy, including many forms of physical touch. Physical touch is a powerful way to communicate your feelings toward your partner and to feel emotionally connected.

Couples who make physical intimacy a priority talk more, communicate better, have more fun, and are generally happier in their relationships. They feel more connected to each other, have more patience, and tend to be more tolerant of the differences in their partner. Overall, they have more positive feelings toward each other and the relationship.

The hormones released during physical intimacy—oxytocin, serotonin, and dopamine—help you feel safe, cared for, and bonded to each other. Oxytocin helps you feel connected to one another and promotes feel-good sensations that create a sense of well-being and happiness. Physical touch also increases levels of dopamine and serotonin, two neurotransmitters that help regulate your mood as well as help your body relieve stress and anxiety. Physical touch can also improve your immune system as well as stoke the desire for more physical connection, making it easier to keep the spark alive in your relationship.

With all these benefits, how do you add more touch to your relationship? It is easier than you think. Awareness is the first step to creating a new habit. Couples can hold hands, hug often, kiss, touch each other while talking, sit next to each other on the couch, snuggle in bed at night, and, yes, have sex when it's right for them. It is the accumulation of touch that matters. The important thing is to touch your partner often, in ways they enjoy.

NO TOUCH, PLEASE

Each individual in a relationship has personal needs for physical touch. These may complement or differ from one's partner in various ways. Some people prefer less of some things and are not comfortable with a great deal of physical touch. If you or your partner falls into this category, it is okay. There are ways to work through this.

1. Begin by having a discussion with your partner in a positive way that does not blame or demand.
2. Let your partner know your desire for physical touch and the reason it is important to you. Knowing the "why" is essential. Offer some examples of how you would like to be touched.
3. Your partner likely will feel differently when they understand your goal is to feel closer and more connected to them, improving your overall relationship.
4. Ask your partner how they enjoy being touched.
5. Are there other behaviors besides touch that make your partner feel loved?
6. Is there something you could do? You might be able to find a common ground where your partner feels comfortable with the touch you desire.
7. Brainstorm ideas without judgment. Coming up with as many ideas as possible will help you identify ways you can both get your needs met.

8. When you show someone love in their preferred way, they are more likely to want to show you love in the way you prefer.

All couples, at various stages, have needs that differ from their partner's. The important thing here is how these issues are discussed and negotiated. Relationships often involve compromise. The goal is to create a solution in which neither person is disappointed and the overall relationship is happy.

Build a Habit

As with other areas of your relationship, life often gets in the way, and physical intimacy can get lost unless you make it a priority. This doesn't have to be difficult. A new habit takes some time and attention to create, but then it becomes part of your regular routine, and you do it without much thought. Let's explore some ways to add this habit to your relationship.

ATTITUDE

Begin with how you show up in the relationship. Your attitude shows through your behavior. If you do not feel the desire for physical connection or if you would like to increase that desire, it starts in your mind. Begin by thinking positive thoughts about your partner. When you remember what you like about them or how you used to feel attracted to them in the beginning of the relationship, your desire to be close will follow. Remind yourself how much you like and appreciate your partner. Spend time anticipating and enjoying physical intimacy. Be open to receiving and giving physical affection.

TALK ABOUT IT

I know this can be a difficult subject for some couples to broach, but I encourage you to open up to your partner. Be honest and let them know how you feel about adding more physical connection to your relationship. Let them know what you like and don't like. You are the only person who knows what feels good to you. Don't hesitate to offer ideas of ways you would like to be touched. Don't be afraid to try new ways of connecting physically and be willing to give your honest opinion afterward. The more you learn about each other, the easier it is to brainstorm ideas and negotiate a solution that meets both your needs.

SET THE STAGE

Don't wait until you are together at the end of the day to start adding more affection to your relationship. It is easier to feel open to intimacy when you set the stage. Create a culture that encourages intimacy. Just because you are partners doesn't mean you can't flirt and have fun with each other. Make it a priority to flirt more with your partner on a regular basis. Now that you are in a relationship, there are no limits to your flirting. You are free to be more daring as long as you both enjoy it. This can be something as simple as whispering in your partner's ear as you hug goodbye in the morning, sending flirty texts during the day, or giving an extra-long kiss when you get back together at the end of the day. Be creative and have fun. Being silly and enjoying fun time together set the stage for relaxing and enjoying intimate activities.

SMALL DAILY ACTS

It is important to set aside time for physical intimacy. You might have to schedule it while first developing the habit. It might sound unromantic, but it is the result that counts. You won't care that you had to schedule time together once you start to reap the results of your actions. Do something intimate every day. The more you touch each other, the more you will want to be intimate. It isn't difficult to add small activities to your day. Try these for starters:

- Hug longer
- Kiss deeper
- Cuddle together while watching TV or reading a book
- Hold hands while you go for a walk
- Take turns giving back or foot rubs
- Rest your hand on your partner's arm or leg
- Give a kiss or hug in passing

Intimacy Needs

It is time to put everything we have talked about into practice.

1. Begin by getting a piece of paper and a pen for each of you.
2. Spend time individually writing a list of ways you enjoy being touched and ways you enjoy touching your partner.
3. Think back to when you were dating; what did you do then?
4. Be bold and add things to your list that you have been thinking about but haven't shared yet.
5. Once you complete your list, get together with your partner and compare.
6. Talk about your need for affection and how it compares with your partner's. This is a great time to brainstorm new ideas.
7. You might also want to share ways your partner can help you get in the mood for more physical touch.
8. Discuss ways to implement the ideas.

Place the ideas into a jar and pick one each day. This is a great way to get in the habit of adding more physical touch to your routine. Start small with one gesture a day and build to spending more time together on a regular basis.

How about scheduling a date night once a week and ending that date exploring new ways to enjoy touch? Set a timer for 10 minutes and take turns touching each other in tender ways. You can experiment with different approaches and see what your partner likes most.

Be open, communicate honestly, make touch a priority, and enjoy the benefits. You might be surprised by what this one small habit can add to your relationship.

CHAPTER 8

SPEND TIME TOGETHER

Spending time together is important in any relationship. Sharing positive experiences strengthens your identification as a couple and builds a greater bond. Spending time together means spending time doing things together, such as common hobbies, time with children, or daily activities. It also includes spending time just *being* together without a specific agenda or activity. The desire to be together is what is important. It is an investment in your relationship as well as time to relax and unwind—something to look forward to.

Be Together

Spending time together is not optional. It is essential for a strong relationship. A common complaint among couples, especially from women, is the lack of quality time spent with a partner. If one partner feels like they don't spend enough time with their partner, it can lead them to question whether they are actually a priority. Lack of time together is a common cause of dissatisfaction in relationships. Connecting often keeps your relationship alive, creating a bond between you. When you spend time together on a regular basis, you see your partner as your support system, the person you can count on, and the place you can go to relax and enjoy life. It increases feelings of self-worth and confidence to know your partner wants to be around you.

Sometimes couples feel that spending time together takes too much effort when they are already tired from all of life's demands. I want you to look at this a new way. It doesn't always have to be something you plan or even a time when you have to talk or make physical contact. What would it be like if you just added time together with no expectations? Time together can mean simply being in the same physical space, just being around each other. Think of it as making a deposit into your emotional bank account.

Time together can help you feel closer and more emotionally connected, which makes it easier to open up and talk to each other and to feel physically attracted to one another. Spending time together sends a message that you like your partner and want to be around them, as you did in the beginning of the relationship. This doesn't mean you have to spend all your free time together. Personal time is also important to couples. The quantity of time isn't as important as the *quality* of time.

Build a Habit

Creating a habit around spending time together doesn't have to be difficult, and it is essential for strengthening your identification as a couple. It starts with making time for each other—finding time in your busy schedule and making it a priority. It can be something as simple as touching base throughout the day with your partner so they know you are thinking of them. Routines can become just that, so we will also discuss keeping your time together fresh and exciting.

MAKE IT A PRIORITY

Life gets busy, and often, couples wait until life slows down to spend time together. We live in a culture where busy is the norm. We think nothing of going about our daily lives doing all the things on our to-do list, forgetting about our relationship with our partner. We assume it will always be there, not realizing how important this one small aspect is to our relationship happiness as a whole. The first step to spending more time together is to make it a priority. Building couple time into your schedule can have a big impact on your happiness level.

SIMPLY TOUCH BASE

Touching base with your partner during the day is a simple and easy way to create a habit of spending more time together. This can be a quick chat in the morning while getting dressed to see what the other person has on their day's agenda. Then check in again when you get home, while making or eating dinner. How about cooking dinner or doing the after-dinner cleanup together? You don't even have to talk if you don't want to; just be together working in the kitchen.

TIME TOGETHER

Be creative about ways to add more time together into your routine. These can be simple things you already do, but now you can do them together, purposefully spending that time with your partner. Relax together in the evening watching your favorite shows, reading a book, or just snuggling on the couch. Make it a priority to share meals together. Add a morning cup of coffee together or a glass of wine after dinner. Spend time relaxing together. It is good for your stress levels and your relationship. How about giving each other a massage or a foot rub? Add a walk after dinner or a drive on the weekend.

TRY SOMETHING NEW

Now that you are adding time together into your daily routine, what about trying something new together? Move outside your comfort zone and try a new activity together. It can be fun. Even if you don't like the activity, you can laugh about trying it, which creates fun memories. Try a new hobby together or maybe even different hobbies you can do at the same time in the same physical space. You are still intentionally setting aside time to be together. I knew a couple that enjoyed doing this: He loved to watch football games, and she liked to knit while he watched the games. They would talk during the commercials, and both felt connected from this activity.

Together Time

Quality time together is more important than the quantity of time as long as you spend enough time to feel connected. The goal is to look forward to connecting with your partner. Be creative, come up with ways you can connect more often with one another. Try something new together, or simply sit in the same room, doing nothing, together. You will find the balance that works for you. Communication is what is important.

Pick a time to sit down with your partner and make a list of all the ideas you can think of to spend time together. This can be a brainstorming session where no ideas are off-limits. Have fun with it.

You can create your lists separately or have fun coming up with ideas together. Either way, once you have a list of ideas, discuss which you would like to try first. Create a combined list and add them to your schedule. I suggest meeting on a regular basis to add to your list and pick new ideas to try.

You can also use this time to check in with how happy your partner is with the amount of time you are spending together and the quality of the time.

Relationships are a journey you take together, and what works at one time might not work at another. As long as you are willing to put time and effort into your connection, you will figure out what works for you at this stage of your relationship.

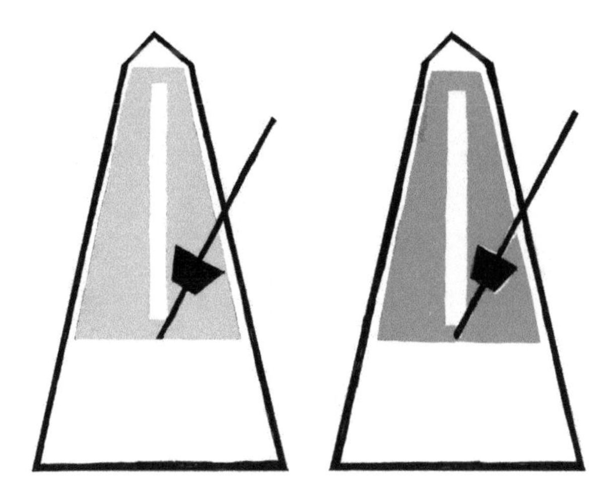

CHAPTER 9

CONNECT THROUGHOUT THE DAY

It is crucial to let your partner know how much they mean to you and that you are thinking of them. Even in good relationships we can be a little insecure and desire that reassurance. It is important to reaffirm throughout the day in different ways that you would choose them again and again. When you make your relationship a daily priority, your partner will feel loved every day. When they feel loved, they will show you more love as well. It is a win–win situation for both. You will increase your emotional and physical connection, leading to a more satisfying and passionate relationship. In this chapter I discuss ways to help you identify where you are feeling disconnected in your relationship. I also offer ideas for connecting throughout the day to feel and stay more connected.

Thinking of Them

It can be hard to find time to stay connected to your partner and keep your relationship a top priority. By the end of a busy day, you may often feel like all you want to do is go to bed, preferably alone, and rest to get ready for the next day. As a result, you and your partner may be left feeling disconnected from one another. If this occurs occasionally, it might not be harmful to the relationship, but when it becomes a habit, it deteriorates your emotional and physical connection as a couple.

Connecting throughout the day doesn't have to take a lot of time or energy, but it can make a big difference in the overall health and happiness of your relationship. Even brief positive exchanges help deepen a couple's emotional connection. Couples can connect in a variety of verbal and nonverbal ways. You can offer support and affection, share humor, or give physical attention. Be intentional in your attitude and actions. This communicates to your partner that they are important to you. It can be something as simple as a smile, a kind word, a flirty text, a passing touch, or saying, "*I love you.*" Small gestures cultivate a feeling of closeness, filling up your emotional bank account.

Feeling more emotionally connected leads to greater feelings of romance and passion, keeping the spark alive in the relationship. Make it a priority to connect with your partner in small ways throughout the day and receive their efforts in return. Connecting and engaging with your partner builds the love, trust, and intimacy vital to a relationship. It is also fun and enjoyable, so why not try it?

Connections Quiz

Take a few minutes to answer the questions in this quiz. Your partner and you should answer the questions separately and then review the results together. It will help you identify where in your relationship you feel disconnected or apathetic. I encourage you not to view this as a negative but as an opportunity to learn more about each other and the ways you can improve your relationship. Later in this chapter you will find ideas to help you connect or reconnect in these areas.

Answer each question with **Very True, Mostly True, Somewhat True,** or **Rarely True.** Use a notebook to record your answers.

1. My partner and I don't feel close anymore, and we don't know how to reconnect.
2. We don't go out on dates with each other as often as I would like.
3. We don't hug, kiss, or touch each other much anymore.
4. My partner doesn't do nice things for me as they used to.
5. We don't have fun together as often as I would like.

6. My partner doesn't compliment me much anymore.
7. I feel as though the spark has gone from our relationship.
8. One or both of us feel bored in our relationship.
9. I don't feel like I am a priority in my partner's life.
10. We don't spend as much time together as I would like.
11. I feel like my partner is not interested in what I have to say or how I feel.
12. My partner doesn't seem to appreciate what I bring to the relationship.
13. We don't laugh together as much as we used to.
14. One or both of us have gotten out of the habit of saying, "I love you."
15. We have gotten out of the habit of reconnecting at the end of the day.

Build a Habit

Now that you have some idea how important it is to connect with your partner throughout the day and you have identified areas where you feel disconnected, it is time to build a habit of connecting. In this section you will learn how to use modern technology to help you stay in touch, making connecting fun and easy. We will explore ways to build a ritual of connection that will fit into any lifestyle. Now is the time to add some fun and playfulness back into your relationship. When was the last time you flirted with your partner? It is time to go back to the beginning when flirting was the norm and you appreciated all the small things your partner did for you. This can be a simple and easy process, so let's get started.

TEXTING

One of the easiest ways to add more connection to your day is using modern technology. How about sending a text message randomly throughout the day telling your partner how much you miss them, how much they mean to you, or that you are thinking of them? You might send a text at lunch that simply says, "*I love you,*" or maybe one that says, "*I can't wait to get home and spend the evening with you.*" Send a text right after you leave the house that says, "*I miss you already.*" Small texts sent on a regular basis are a great way of staying connected throughout the day.

DAILY CALL

Another idea is to call your partner before you leave work for the day. Check in to ask whether you can do anything for them on the way home. Take care of personal business items so you can focus more on relaxing or having fun when you are home.

RECONNECT AT THE END OF THE DAY

Once you are home, find time to give your partner your full attention. Ask about their day and really listen to the answer. Turn off all devices and cuddle on the couch holding hands while you share with each other. Let your partner know how happy you are to be together. Use this time to share what is going on in your life. Couples can feel disconnected when they keep problems or issues to themselves. Your partner is there to support you, so talk to them and let them help. Take time to snuggle in bed together before going to sleep. Ending your day feeling emotionally close will help you stay connected and add more passion to your physical relationship.

FLIRT

In the beginning of a relationship, people tend to do a lot more flirting. It is time to go back to that. You can flirt in person, leave notes, or flirt in your daily texts. Make it fun and enjoyable. Tell your partner how nice they look in the morning before you part for work. Let them know you look forward to spending time together that evening. Send a text that says, "*I am counting the hours until I see you again.*" You can also send flirty memes to your partner. When was the last time you winked at your partner or gave them a quick kiss as you passed by? If your partner is appreciative, send sexy texts or add some teasing to your flirting for fun.

GRATITUDE

This is another area often overlooked as relationships progress. Spend time daily letting your partner know you appreciate them and what they do for you and for your family. Don't forget to say, "Thank you." Tell them why they are a great partner. Show gratitude for the little things they do on a daily basis. It will make them feel loved, appreciated, and recognized. Tell your partner you are proud of them and let them know why. Compliment them not only on their looks but also on their character. Once you begin to notice and share gratitude, you will find even more to be grateful for.

Spark a Reconnection

Spending time together is something to look forward to and enjoy. Look over the following ideas and pick a new one to try daily or weekly depending on your schedule. You might add this to your weekly date night. Make note of other ideas as they come to you. Once you get started, you will find more ways to make this a habit you enjoy.

» Spend some time together looking at old photos and enjoy reminiscing.

» Watch a funny movie and enjoy laughing together.

» Pack a picnic and enjoy the meal and time in nature.

» Write your partner a love note and leave it for them to find.

» Hold hands while you go for an evening walk.

» Recreate your first date and enjoy a "first date" all over again.

» Take a day off work and vacation together in your own town or in your own home.

» Spend an evening holding hands, looking into each other's eyes, and kissing like you did when you were first dating.

- Share memories of your favorite vacations or times together as a couple.
- Exercise together.
- Spend time talking about your dreams for the future—where you want to live, trips you want to take, or things you want to do.
- Give each other a massage. It can be as simple as a shoulder or foot rub.
- Sit together in the park and enjoy watching people pass by.
- Play a board game together, maybe one of your favorites from childhood.
- Cook a meal together. This is a great time to try something new.
- Put on your favorite music and dance together. This can be fun, romantic, or both.
- Leave a note that has "I love you" written in different languages.
- Book a night at a local hotel just for the evening.

CHAPTER 10

LISTEN TO ONE ANOTHER

Communication can be one of the most effective ways to create and maintain a strong, healthy relationship. Giving your partner your undivided attention and really listening to what they have to say, what they think, and how they feel make up one of the most important habits you can develop in your relationship. Without good communication, it is easy for couples to become frustrated and feel alone in the relationship. Concentrate on hearing what the other person says, not just listening to prepare a response. Active listening is about making a conscious decision to really listen to our partner with the goal of understanding. In this chapter you will learn what it means to actively listen to your partner and why this skill is so important to the overall happiness of your relationship. You will also learn how to listen so your partner feels heard and understood.

Active Listening

When your partner speaks, do you really listen? Often, we think we are, but our mind is already planning our response before they even finish talking. Couples often complain that all they want is for their partner to hear them, but instead, what they get is advice for solving the problem. By listening, your partner will feel better and may even come up with their own solution. There is a time to offer ideas, but this is not it.

After your partner shares, you could let them know you have some ideas that might be helpful and ask whether now is a good time to share those. If they say, "No, thank you," honor their decision and let them know you are always available to help. Active listening is not about problem solving; it is about creating a safe space for your partner to feel heard and supported. This is the time to listen without judgment, give your undivided attention, and ask clarifying questions for more information when appropriate. Not only listen to their words but also be attentive to their emotions.

Learning to listen and having empathy are indications of a good communicator. The importance of listening to your partner cannot be overemphasized. It is the basis of every healthy relationship. When we listen, we tell our partner we care about their thoughts and feelings. Often, all that is needed is to let your partner know you are there to support them. Using active listening is a great way to avoid misunderstandings, build an emotional connection, and create a habit of sharing and supporting each other.

Build a Habit

Now that you have an idea of what active listening is and how important it is to your relationship, let's talk more about how to incorporate it into your communication. Learning how to hear each other is a skill you can improve with practice. It is important to pick the right time and place to have these conversations and to stick to one topic at a time. What you say is important, but equally important are how you say it and what your body language conveys.

TIME AND PLACE

It is important to pick the right time and place to have conversations. Don't ask your partner to listen to you when they first walk in the door after a long day at work or while watching their favorite TV show. You probably will not get the reaction you want. Make sure you both have time for an uninterrupted conversation. This is not a time to multitask.

Pick a location where there are minimal distractions and you won't be interrupted. You may need to let your partner know you want to discuss something and ask if it is a good time. If your partner starts talking and you cannot give them your attention, it is okay to let them know how important it is to you to listen to them and then plan a time that works for you both. It is better to wait than to have an unsatisfactory conversation. Just be sure to follow through at the designated time.

CHOOSE A TOPIC

It is important to choose your topic and stick to that topic. Long conversations that go around and around with no end in sight are not beneficial. If you are the one initiating the conversation, stick to one main point. You can have another conversation later. The goal is to make this a satisfactory experience for both people, encouraging future conversations. Often, one topic leads to another and the conversation can get off track with no one feeling heard or understood. You will also want to avoid bringing up the past. This is usually counterproductive to the current conversation. The other person can become defensive and stop listening. One topic at a time that focuses on the here and now will increase the likelihood of a positive outcome.

HOW YOU SAY IT MATTERS

What you say, the tone you use, and your body language while talking are all important. Put down any devices and make eye contact with each other. Lean in toward your partner to let them know you are engaged. Be careful not to sit with your arms crossed or to fidget with something in your hands. Doing so can send the message you aren't paying attention. Both of you should pay attention to the tone you use. Do you sound angry, bored, or interested? This makes a difference. Sometimes how you say something and the specific words you use can determine the outcome of the conversation. Remember to avoid making judgments or giving unsolicited advice. Feel free to ask questions to learn more or to clarify your understanding. If your partner is upset about a situation, it is okay to ask how you can help.

END WITH A POSITIVE

Once you feel like your partner has said all they need to, ask if there is anything else. Make sure the conversation really is over. I suggest ending the conversation with something positive, such as a hug or a kiss. Doing so will bring positive closure to the discussion and serve as a sign you can move forward. It will help you both feel good about the experience and encourage future conversations.

Listen Together

To help improve your active listening skills and encourage you to make active listening a habit in your relationship, try the following exercise.

1. Pick an agreed-upon time and place when and where you will not be distracted.
2. Set a timer for 10 minutes.
3. Decide who will go first and let that person pick a topic they want to discuss.
4. Use all the skills you have learned in this chapter to actively listen to your partner.
5. When the timer goes off, reset it for 10 more minutes and switch roles.
6. After you both have been the listener and the one who shares, spend some time discussing what the experience was like.
    - Did you feel heard and understood?
    - How did it feel to listen to your partner?
    - Avoid any judgments in this conversation.
    - Remember, you are both learning and improving a skill.

- Let the other person know what they did right and give any suggestions for improvement in a kind way.
- Let each other know how good it felt to be heard.

The more you practice, the more trust you will build, the easier the conversations will become, and the more emotional intimacy you will develop.

CHAPTER 11

MANAGE CONFLICT AND COMPROMISE

Disagreements and conflict are inevitable in relationships. They can lead to the deterioration of the relationship or they can become a source of growth. Your ability to handle issues when they arise, manage conflict, and come to a resolution is essential for any long-term relationship. Not only are disagreements inevitable, but they can be good for the relationship when handled correctly. In this chapter we will take a deeper look at conflict, ways to manage it, how to compromise when necessary, and how to create a habit of conflict resolution that is empowering to you and your relationship.

Conflict Resolution

Two people come together in a relationship with different backgrounds, life experiences, personalities, ideas, and viewpoints. It is easy to see why conflicts are inevitable. When left unresolved, they are harmful to any relationship. When you fight against each other, no one wins. Conflict itself isn't a problem. How you deal with conflict can be. When addressed in a positive way, issues can help you learn more about your partner and lead to feeling closer. Knowing you can resolve any problem together that arises increases your emotional connection. In a healthy relationship both partners are free to express themselves without fearing the other person's reaction.

Now that you have practiced active listening skills in chapter 10 (if you haven't, take time to review them now), it is time to take listening a step further and learn to resolve conflicts in a positive way. Yes, it is possible to learn this skill together. You can learn to discuss issues that arise without accusing or attacking your partner. You can learn to take responsibility for your actions when appropriate and discuss options that will benefit the partnership as a whole. To do this, you need to create a new habit around conflict resolution.

Give and Take

Learning to give and take can be one of the most difficult things to do in a relationship. But doing so is an essential part of conflict resolution and living happily together as a couple. It is always easier to see issues from your point of view and find reasons you are correct as well as why the other person should see it your way. The need to be right is something everyone must deal with from time to time. We can all become stubborn and even demanding in thoughts and actions. This is understandable, but it is necessary to be able to move beyond our own views to work as a successful team. When we are not able to see the other person's point of view, we have a tendency to become either demanding or critical, which will automatically put the other person on the defensive. This adds roadblocks to productive problem-solving conversations and makes it more difficult to come up with solutions. You end up in battle mode instead of working together as a team.

Build a Habit

It is important to learn to manage conflict when it arises in a way that creates closeness rather than separation. How would you feel about your partner and your relationship if you knew you could handle any conflict that arises and were confident you could come to a compromise that works for you both? How would this improve your relationship? It is time to find out. Learning to "fight fair" is essential in any relationship.

THE RIGHT TIME

It starts with choosing the right time and place to have a conversation with your loved one. What tends to happen is that we become upset about something and want to share those feelings immediately. This is not, generally, the best idea. If your emotions are running high, make sure you have time to cool down to get ready for a conversation. It is difficult to think clearly when you are upset. When you communicate out of anger, you are more likely to say things that only add to the issue. Doing so leads to more frustration and causes one or both parties to become even more upset. So, first calm down, and then pick a time when you and your partner can give the conversation your full attention. By giving yourself time and space before you talk, you may find more clarity on what is truly bothering you.

GET TO THE HEART OF THE ISSUE

What is really bothering you that needs to be addressed? Often, there is something deeper than the original issue at hand. For example, if you are upset that your partner is late for a date night, there may be more to it than just being late for a dinner reservation. Their running late might suggest to you that they do not make the relationship a priority. The conversation might be better served by addressing your need to feel like a priority instead of being late for a date night.

I encourage you to take time to decide what is bothering you and what topic you want to discuss to make the most of your time together. Then be sure to stick to that one topic. Bringing up the past, making laundry lists of things that are bothering you, or loading it on in heaps isn't helpful; it usually deteriorates the conversation and stops the progress you are trying to achieve.

PAY ATTENTION TO BODY LANGUAGE

Sometimes we focus solely on what is being said and not on *how* it is being said. You can learn so much more information when you pay attention to nonverbal communication such as body language and facial expressions. Up to half of what we convey to others comes from nonverbal communication. Being aware of how you convey information and watching the other person's body language can help you resolve conflict in a more productive way. Some things to look for and avoid are crossed arms, pointing a finger at the other person, avoiding eye contact, making angry facial expressions, or not giving the other person enough personal space. It's also of great importance to take note of tone of voice. Avoid a loud or harsh tone. All these are signs that you or the other person is not in a receptive space for problem solving. Instead, aim for a relaxed posture, even breathing, and an open stance, showing willingness to share and receive information.

SET BOUNDARIES

While discussing an issue, it is important to set boundaries. We already talked about addressing one topic at a time and sticking to the present. However, don't forget the golden rule of conflict resolution: Everyone deserves to be heard and treated with respect. No one should feel attacked, and the conversation should not lower anyone's self-esteem. You are a team, and the goal is to find a resolution that will enhance your relationship, not harm it.

LISTEN AND VALIDATE

Listen with the goal of understanding what the real issue is. Remember, sometimes it is not the original problem but rather a deeper issue that needs to be addressed for real resolution to occur. When one person in the relationship becomes upset, there is always an unmet need. The start to the solution is to identify that need. Learning to identify and discuss the real issue helps avoid future conflict. Are you really upset that your partner didn't do a certain chore around the house, or are you feeling overwhelmed by the amount of responsibility you have for running the household? Listen and ask questions to get to the bottom of what is going on. Be sure to validate each other's feelings. You don't have to feel the same way to understand that your partner might have different needs and wants.

BRAINSTORM OPTIONS TOGETHER

Brainstorming together can help you come up with an idea you might not think of alone. When you brainstorm, no idea is a bad idea. There might be times when the best outcome is to agree to disagree. Other times you can come up with a win-win solution. This might take some time and patience and you may have to come back to it after thinking about possible solutions. Not every situation will have an immediate resolution. You might need to do some research or just have time to process before you talk again. People process information in different ways. Some do so by having discussions, but others need time alone. It is okay to agree to take time out and come back to discuss the issue further. When you both are willing to listen, hear the other person, and be open to new ideas, you can find a way to compromise on most issues. Remember, relationships are a work in progress, and they constantly change and evolve.

Scripting Resolution

In this exercise a couple has received an unexpected amount of money from a work bonus, and the partners do not agree on how to spend the money. One person wants to save it, and the other wants to take a nice vacation. The following is a sample script to show how they might resolve this conflict. This is a short version to give you an idea of the principles we have discussed in this chapter. Obviously, in real life it might require more discussion than is shown here.

After you have chosen a time and place to have the discussion that works for you both, agree on a set time limit for the exercise (10 to 15 minutes). This helps keep you both on task and focused on the topic and solution.

Read the script, with each of you reading one of the partner's responses:

Partner A: *"I am so excited about the money we got! I am looking forward to taking that dream trip we have been talking about for so long. But I am disappointed and frustrated that now that we have money you don't want to go. I feel as though if we don't go now, when we have this money, we won't ever go. Having experiences together is important to me."*

Partner B: *"I understand that having experiences together is important to you, and I realize we have been discussing this dream trip for a while now. I can see how you might feel frustrated by my desire to put the money into savings instead of taking a trip."*

At this point, both partners can take turns sharing more about why their positions are important to them. Be sure to validate the other person's point of view without judgment. For example:

Partner A: *"I understand you are looking out for our future by adding to our savings. Is there a way we can do both?"*

Take time to brainstorm compromises. Discuss how much money you are comfortable spending on a different trip and how much would go into savings. This is a win-win. An example might be:

Partner A: *"I can see the benefit of putting money into savings. What if we take a smaller trip and spend only some of the money with the rest going into savings?"*

Partner B: *"I would be okay with that. Do you have an idea of a trip that would fit into the new budget and still make you happy?"*

Discuss options for trips. It can be a bonding experience to start a new dream together. You could research ideas individually and get back together to plan a new destination, both feeling good about the compromise.

CHAPTER 12

SHARE TRADITIONS

Routines are important, even for couples. Creating routines they enjoy helps a couple feel secure in their relationship. It strengthens their bond and gives them something to anticipate. Spending time together is important for creating and keeping the emotional and physical bond between two people. Creating routines ensures that you spend quality time together. This can include daily morning and evening routines as well as weekend and holiday traditions. In this chapter we will look at why shared traditions are important to your relationship. You will work on building small traditions into your routine, making this time together something you automatically do and look forward to.

Create Rituals

Rituals help make relationships a priority, creating and maintaining deep emotional connections with your partner. Participating in something that holds meaning for you both creates a bond between you. It is important to make an effort every day to connect with each other so it becomes second nature. Having rituals increases your emotional well-being and creates a memory bank of happy, healthy experiences. Your memory bank strengthens your relationship and makes it easier to deal with those inevitable times of stress. Be open and imaginative when creating rituals. You might be surprised by how much you look forward to these new habits. Each couple is unique, so take the ideas from this chapter, try different ones, and develop some of your own to create rituals that work for you. The important thing is to make whatever you choose a routine you both can count on and look forward to.

Build a Habit

With all the distractions in life, it is easy for couples to grow distant from each other over time. Relationships require conscious action, which is much easier to do when you have routines in place that support your efforts. By creating opportunities to connect on a regular basis, you ensure that you keep your relationship a top priority. It doesn't have to be difficult when you create habits and rituals.

CREATE ROUTINES

It is time to create a new habit and add new ways of connecting to your day. You might already do some of these things; if so, continue, but also be willing to add new routines. These are meant to be easy and fun, with the goal of creating enjoyable moments in your relationship. The idea is to come up with a set of routines you establish that mean something to both of you and that you carry out on a regular basis. I encourage you to do things daily, weekly, or monthly. This will take some discussion to ensure that you participate in activities you both enjoy. Often couples think they are doing things that are meaningful to their partner but find out later that their partner prefers something else. If we put effort into our relationship, we want it to be meaningful effort. Be sure to have an open discussion around these routines. Your partner will happily offer ideas if you need them.

SPEAK THEIR LOVE LANGUAGE

We all have different ways we prefer to show and receive love, and we want to show love to our partner in a way they prefer. Gary Chapman wrote a book called *The 5 Love Languages* that explains how couples can express and experience their language of love and affection. According to Chapman, these are the five love languages:

1. Words of affirmation
2. Physical touch
3. Quality time
4. Receiving gifts
5. Acts of service

You might want to take the online love language quiz to learn more about your and your partner's preferences by searching "five languages of love quiz." This doesn't mean you only show love to your partner in one or two ways, but it can help you develop ideas for new shared rituals meaningful to both people.

DAILY ROUTINES

To establish a new routine, you need to implement the activity on a regular basis. The easiest way to do this is to create daily habits that allow you to connect throughout the day. For example, consider a morning connection routine. You might have coffee or breakfast together, and then share a goodbye hug and kiss. Midday you might send each other a funny or flirty text. At the end of the day, you might make dinner together and spend time sharing about your day while you unwind. Can you see how easy it is to create daily bonding moments? You can also add weekly or monthly routines into your plan, such as date nights.

TACKLE THE LIST

Write down a plan, try it for a week or so, and then modify it as needed. Check in with each other periodically to see if the routine is still working for both people. You can always try new things or modify as life or individual needs change. The important part is to create the routine so it stays a priority and you consistently share positive experiences.

New Traditions

Review the following list together and highlight ideas you want to try; then brainstorm others to add to the list. Once you have a list of ideas, talk about which you will implement first and come up with a plan for daily ideas, weekly ideas, and monthly or special-occasion traditions to implement. If this is a new idea for you, start simple and add more ideas as you go. Remember, you can always make changes and incorporate new ideas. I encourage you to check in with each other periodically to reevaluate.

- Discuss your upcoming day while getting ready together in the morning.
- Leave hidden love notes for the other person to find.
- Reconnect during the day with a quick text or send a meaningful meme.
- Compliment your partner at least once daily.
- Run errands together on the weekend.
- Take a walk together in the evening or go on a weekend hike.
- Make dinner or do the dishes together and catch up on daily events.

- Reconnect in the evening with a hug and kiss—make it at least a 10-second kiss to start the hormones flowing.
- Plan a weekly date night, which can be an outing or time spent together at home.
- Express appreciation daily for something your partner does or something they add to your life.
- Turn off everything and spend time just being together.
- Plan a monthly getaway, just the two of you.
- Go to bed at the same time so you have time to relax together at the end of every day.
- Set your alarm 10 minutes earlier and snuggle before you start your day.
- Find a hobby you can share together.

CHAPTER 13

ACCEPT YOUR PARTNER

A big part of having a successful relationship is maintaining reasonable expectations. We all come into relationships with beliefs of how a relationship should work and how a partner should act. These beliefs come from our family of origin and past experiences. The problem is that we may not have the same expectations our partner does. We may not even know these expectations exist, yet we act on them. This can lead to complaining, criticizing, and arguing. In this chapter we will talk about how to accept your partner for who they are. We are all imperfect humans doing the best we can. When we see this in ourselves and in our partner, we create amazing loving relationships.

Practice Acceptance

At the beginning of the relationship, we see our partner through rose-colored glasses. They seem perfect, without flaws; even when they show imperfections, we overlook them or make excuses for them. We are full of those feel-good hormones and have a vested interest in wanting them to be perfect so we can move forward in the relationship. As time passes, you may be shocked to learn your partner isn't perfect.

In reality, no one changed. The fog of love lifted, and you began to see your partner as they truly are. Even though it feels as though they have changed, it's your perception of them that has changed. The small things you found cute or endearing may start to drive you crazy. This can lead to wanting to change your partner: They are perfect if only they would change a few small things. You might begin to complain and criticize, which leads to arguments and hurt feelings. This is also the stage when couples start to realize their relationship expectations may not be realistic. They might expect their partner to always agree with them or act in a way and make decisions they agree with. They might fall into the belief that everything would be perfect if the other person would just make some changes.

The key to a happy relationship is radical acceptance of your partner for who they are—flaws and all. After all, what you see as a flaw someone else might see as a desirable trait. When you begin to accept each other as the perfectly imperfect person for you, your relationship can evolve into one of mutual respect and deep love.

Build a Habit

This might sound good, but I know you are wondering, *How in the world do I see my partner's imperfections in a positive light?* Going from criticism and arguing to creating a deeper bond is a skill you learn, moving toward acceptance, compassion, respect, and understanding of your partner for who they are, quirks and all. With practice, you can learn to turn your thoughts around and see each other in a new, more positive light. This next section will start your journey to creating this new habit.

ACCEPTANCE

Learning to accept your partner for who they are, quirks and all, is essential. Too often we tolerate certain behaviors or traits in our partner, which is not the same as acceptance. Acceptance means you see and love them as a whole person. This doesn't mean you have to like everything about them, but you do allow them to be who they are. You accept their wants and needs as uniquely theirs and do your best to work together as a couple.

COMPASSION

Do your best to strive to have compassion and empathy for each other. Instead of judging the way your partner thinks or acts, work on turning those thoughts to gratitude. For example, instead of judging the way your partner loads the dishwasher, find gratitude in the fact that they help with the dishes. Does it really matter how the dishwasher gets loaded as long as the dishes are clean in the end? It starts by becoming aware of your thoughts and judgments so you can decide whether these are beneficial to your relationship or whether it would be better to look at the situation in a new light.

RESPECT

Respect is such an important part of any good relationship. You will never agree on everything. It's not a realistic expectation. Instead of trying to control the other person, you can learn to respect their difference in opinions and actions. Remember, you do not always have to agree with each other. You can learn to listen and acknowledge your partner's thoughts and opinions and respect that they have a right to them. Give your partner the respect and understanding that you would like in return.

UNDERSTANDING

Understanding comes when you begin to learn more about your partner: why they think and act the way they do. They might have experiences and beliefs you do not understand. When you take time to learn more about them, this understanding leads to acceptance and respect. Unconditional love is the ultimate goal for most of us. To know you are loved and accepted by your partner for who you are is the greatest gift you can give and receive.

SEE THE POSITIVES

It is important to remember why you fell in love in the first place. Learn to see the positives in the differences. Sometimes those differences in your partner provide the perfect balance to your personality. You each have different strengths, and often, they complement each other. When you focus on the small things you don't like, you might miss all the good your partner contributes to your life and relationship. Learn to accept your partner's imperfections and see the blessings in them.

Let Me Count the Ways

When life gets busy, we sometimes forget what attracted us to the other person in the first place. What was it that you noticed and that attracted you to them through the noise and craziness of daily life?

For this exercise, I encourage you to make a list of all the things you like and love about your partner:

- List all the good qualities you see in your partner, all they bring to the relationship and all they add to your life.
- Think back and remember what you first liked about your partner.
- What have you learned since the beginning of the relationship that makes your partner a good choice?

Ask your partner to do the same, if they are willing. Get together and share your lists with each other. You can do this all at once, or you can share one thing each day. Keep the list handy so when you need to shift your focus, you can refer to it as a reminder. Add to it as you think of new things.

When you find yourself noticing negative thought patterns regarding your partner, you now have a way to turn those thoughts around. Remember, the ultimate goal is to accept your partner as a whole person. Being able to look at a list of the positives can help you put things in perspective. This is also the time to remember compassion and empathy. Put yourself in their shoes. How do you want to be treated? Do you want them to accept you, quirks and flaws included? Give each other respect and watch your relationship flourish.

CHAPTER 14

HAPPILY EVER AFTER

Too often people in relationships believe that if they are with the right person, their relationship will be easy and they will not have to work to keep the connection they first had. They may also have unrealistic expectations of relationships in general. Not only are these beliefs impractical, but they can also be damaging to any relationship. You can have an amazing relationship, and you deserve that relationship, but it requires working on your connection with your partner. This is a vital part of the equation for experiencing a stronger, more intimate bond. In this chapter we will look at the myth of happily ever after and ideas for breaking negative cycles as well as ways to rekindle the passion. Great relationships are possible when you put in the effort and recommit to your partner on a daily basis with intention and actions.

The Myth of Happily Ever After

A myth is a widely held belief or idea. Myths are not individual ideas but collective attitudes held by society and passed from generation to generation. We rarely question them and take them as truths; we might not even realize we have them.

When it comes to relationships, a myth is something a lot of people believe but that is generally unsustainable. A common myth is that happy couples do not fight. Society perpetuates the myth that happy couples always get along. That is not realistic. You and your partner are not always going to see eye to eye. What is important is that you can speak the truth in a kind and loving way, using disagreements to strengthen your bond.

Some common relationship myths include:

- My partner should know what I want and need without my having to tell them.
- If our relationship is good, we won't argue or fight.
- My partner should always be available when I need them.
- Good relationships are easy.

When you begin to look at your beliefs and expectations, you can question their validity. This will open you to new possibilities. Relationships require flexibility and a willingness to see the other person's perspective and work together for solutions. You are constantly changing and evolving, as is with your partner. That means your relationship has to evolve as well. For relationships to thrive, you must stay open and flexible.

The concept of "happily ever after" isn't real, no matter how many movies and bedtime stories tell us otherwise. So many people believe choosing the right partner is all you need to be happy. Then, when the honeymoon phase (inevitably) ends, they become disappointed and may even believe they have to settle for an unhappy relationship. The truth is there is no such thing as the perfect relationship or the perfect partner. No one is perfect, and two imperfect people do not make a perfect relationship.

Relationships are wonderful opportunities to grow and learn about yourself and as a couple. With patience, caring, and commitment, you can create and maintain a happy relationship.

Break the Negative Cycle

You cannot be in a long-term relationship without arguing from time to time. But some couples fall into a pattern of negativity and find themselves constantly bickering with no real resolution. In my experience, I have found that most couples argue over small things. They become irritated by beliefs, behaviors, and small quirks they find annoying. These might even be things thought cute at the beginning of the relationship but that now they want their partner to change. These small things can bother anyone, but couples in healthy relationships know how to handle this situation in a productive way. Let's look at how to break this negative cycle.

STOP BLAMING

The first step is to stop blaming each other. You are not really upset because your partner was late or because they forgot to take the trash out. You are upset because you allowed their behavior to upset you. I know taking responsibility for your emotions is not always an easy thing to do, but when you can look at your irritation in this new way, you have control over your feelings and actions. What your partner says or does no longer determines how you feel. This doesn't mean you cannot have a discussion with them about issues that come up.

It means these discussions can be productive, not arguments where you blame each other and resolve nothing. Start by taking responsibility for your part in the situation. What upsets you might not upset someone else, so your partner may not even see their actions as irritating.

PRACTICE CONFLICT RESOLUTION

One of the most important aspects of resolving issues is to address them in a timely manner. I suggest that you don't discuss an issue while your emotions are heightened. Allow some time to pass so you can calm down and think about what you want to say and what you would like the resolution to be. Be careful not to wait too long, though. Often, when couples begin to discuss one issue, it turns into an argument about the last five things that upset one of them. Be careful not to sit on resentment and let it fester until you blow up over something small.

For these conversations to go well, it is important to avoid certain attitudes and behaviors. In Dr. John Gottman's book *The Seven Principles for Making Marriage Work,* he talks about the toxicity of becoming defensive and showing contempt. This might include eye-rolling, ridiculing, name-calling, or sarcasm.

State your needs in a positive way, taking responsibility for your feelings and desires. Make sure you hear each other and acknowledge each other's views and feelings. This helps you stay out of the negative cycle of blaming the other person and resolving nothing. When you communicate in a positive way and express your views as your own, it opens the door for your partner to listen and hear you. Then you can discuss a resolution that will work for both of you.

INCREASE AFFECTION

When couples come to me because they are not getting along, one of the first things I ask about is their level of intimacy and physical affection toward one other. What I usually hear is that they are not being affectionate because they are not getting along. I understand how they feel, but I want to suggest to you what I suggest to them. By increasing your level of affection, you will automatically feel more patient, appreciative, and forgiving toward each other.

Schedule time to share physical intimacy, even if you don't feel like it. Start by remembering what you do like about your partner. Positive thoughts help you feel more positive, which makes it easier to be affectionate. Start small with deliberate hugs or just snuggling on the couch. Once you get started, chances are you will enjoy the experience. Physical contact releases oxytocin, which we talked about earlier as the bonding hormone. This hormone causes you to see the other person in a more positive light. It is beneficial to your relationship in a variety of ways.

FOCUS ON THE POSITIVE

Where your thoughts go, feelings follow. When you focus on the little things you do not like about your partner, you notice them more. The opposite is also true; when you focus on the positives, you are happier with your partner. It takes the same amount of effort, so why not put your attention on things that will help create and maintain a happy loving relationship? When you actively work on building positivity in your relationship, there will be less arguing and bickering. I suggest making a list of all the things you like about your partner—why did you choose them in the first place? Keep this list on your phone and add to it when you notice something else you appreciate. Once your focus goes to the positives, you begin to see more to be grateful for. Keep this list handy so when your thoughts stray toward the negative, you can review it and remind yourself why you love your partner.

FIND COMMON GROUND

A common belief in relationships is that you have to win an argument for it to be successful. Remember, the relationship as a whole is what is important. You don't always have to be right or win. The goal is to understand each other's points of view and needs. From this point of connection, you can begin to discuss options with a focus on finding common ground during an argument rather than winning. Be willing to look beyond who is right and embrace the possibility of new solutions you have not yet thought of. Sometimes you will decide it is okay for one partner to have their way, and sometimes you will need to work on a compromise you can both agree on.

Rekindle the Flame

So far, you have learned a great deal about what makes a relationship work and the healthy habits you can form to build and grow a loving relationship. Now, it is time to take a closer look at what your ideal relationship would look like. It is beneficial to look periodically at where you are and where you would like to be with your intimate partner. Take some time to reflect on what that ideal relationship looks like to each of you. Everyone has their own version of an ideal relationship. How does your current relationship compare to this ideal? This reflection will highlight areas of the book you might want to go back and reread. Where do you need to put in some time and effort to move toward your ideal?

Relationships can start great but, over time, lose some of what makes them special. It takes effort to keep the spark alive. Following are some ideas of ways to rekindle the flame in your relationship. I suggest doing some or all of these, even if you have a good relationship. Relationships require nurturing, and there is always room for growth and improvement.

GIVING AND RECEIVING

Giving your partner attention and being willing to receive what they offer make up a wonderful dance couples do together. They take turns leading and following. Giving attention makes your partner feel loved and cared for. It is a wonderful opportunity to learn more about each other, strengthening the emotional bond between you. It also provides a sense of security, knowing you can count on the other person and that you always have each other to lean on.

I encourage you to set up a routine where you take turns listening to each other, sharing about your day. Take turns with physical affection and other ways of giving and receiving the love important to you as a couple. Remember, people feel loved in different ways, so you do not need to give in the same ways as long as you both feel the other person is putting their best effort into the relationship.

TRUST AND RESPECT

Each person in a relationship needs to feel valued and cared for. No one wants to feel taken for granted. Trust and respect are two of the most important ingredients in a relationship. This means being conscious that your words and actions match. If you say you are going to do something, do it. Showing you can be trusted allows your partner to relax and connect with you on a deeper level.

Respect is equally important. This means respecting your partner as an individual, allowing them to have different views and opinions without judgment—not only loving them but also liking them for who they are. Tell your partner, not just once but often, how much you love and care for them. This goes a long way in keeping or rekindling the flame in a relationship.

ENVISION A FUTURE

As a couple, it is important to look forward and envision a future together. This creates a sense of security and gives you common goals to work toward. This might mean envisioning financial goals, vacation plans, emotional relationship goals, or something as simple as your next date night. Whatever is meaningful to you as a couple is where you can put your attention. You might want to write down your goals or vision and revisit them periodically to make changes and help you stay on course. Working together toward common goals increases your friendship and connection as a couple. Seeing yourself happily together in the future reaffirms your commitment to one another.

(Re)Committing to One Another

Congratulations! You have invested time and energy in reading this book and implementing some of its suggestions. You are on your way to creating new habits that will have a long-term positive impact on your relationship. Small steps taken on a daily basis will continue to build your connection and increase your happiness. By reading this book and creating new habits, you show yourself and your partner that you are committed to a long-term, loving relationship where you grow together as a team. Building and maintaining loving relationships takes effort and commitment, but the results are worth it.

Throughout this book you have learned what it takes to develop a stronger, more intimate relationship. You have learned the importance of creating a common vision so you can work together as a team. This goes a long way toward managing conflict with a common goal of creating a win–win situation. It is important to let go of your need to be right. Instead, keep the relationship your top priority. You have learned to be curious about your partner. There is always something new to learn. When you listen to one another, you not only connect emotionally but also keep the spark alive. We also talked about the importance of being kind and thoughtful with your partner. You have begun to create new habits of connecting with each other daily, accepting your partner for who they are while sharing special times together, emotionally and physically.

Trying to reconnect and rekindle your relationship takes time, but if you are both committed, it will happen. Remember, you fell in love with each other and made a commitment to be together for a reason. This commitment is not a one-time event. Happy relationships require making a decision to commit and recommit to your partner every day.

Now, I encourage you to continue to follow through with the habits you have started. I suggest revisiting sections of the book, one at a time, and making a commitment to try new things, make new habits, and refine what you have learned. Each time you read a chapter you will gain new insights and spark your imagination for ways to implement the ideas. Keep your shared relationship goals in mind as you move forward together, one step and one day at a time, creating the relationship you desire and deserve.

RESOURCES

BOOKS

Getting the Love You Want by Harville Hendrix

Love & Respect by Emerson Eggerichs

Making Marriage Simple by Harville Hendrix and Helen LaKelly Hunt

Radical Marriage by David and Darlene Steele

The Seven Principles for Making Marriage Work by John M. Gottman and Nan Silver

Wabi Sabi Love by Arielle Ford

WEBSITES

Gottman Institute: Gottman.com

HuffPost: HuffPost.com/life/relationships

National Domestic Violence Hotline: TheHotline.org

Psychology Today: PsychologyToday.com/us

The 5 Love Languages: 5LoveLanguages.com

REFERENCES

Chapman, Gary. *The 5 Love Languages*. Chicago: Northfield Publishing, 2015.

Chin, B., M. Murphy, D. Janicki-Deverts, and S. Cohen. "Marital Status as a Predictor of Diurnal Salivary Cortisol Levels and Slopes in a Community Sample of Healthy Adults." *Psychoneuro-endocrinology* 78 (April 2017): 68–75. doi.org/10.1016/j.psyneuen.2017.01.016.

Edwards, Scott. "Love and the Brain." *On the Brain* (Harvard Mahoney Neuroscience Institute). March 2015. Neuro.HMS.Harvard.edu/harvard-mahoney-neuroscience-institute/brain-newsletter/and-brain/love-and-brain.

Gottman, John M., and Nan Silver. *The Seven Principles for Making Marriage Work*. New York: Harmony, 1999.

Gunn, H. E., D. J. Buysse, B. P. Hasler, A. Begley, and W. M. Troxel. "Sleep Concordance in Couples is Associated with Relationship Characteristics." *Sleep* 38, no. 6 (June 2015): 933–39. doi:10.5665/sleep.4744.

Harvard Health Letter. "Can Relationships Boost Longevity and Well-Being?" Harvard Health Publishing, Harvard Medical School. June 2017. Health.Harvard.edu/mental-health/can-relationships-boost-longevity-and-well-being.

INDEX

ACKNOWLEDGMENTS

I want to first thank Callisto Media for allowing me the privilege of authoring this book.

I thank my amazing and loving father and grandparents who first showed me what real love really is. They were living examples of what is possible in life and love. Even though they are no longer with me, they are part of my life and have contributed to this book.

I appreciate all my wonderful friends, colleagues, and clients who provided support and encouragement throughout this process. I have an amazing support system that cheers me on anytime I mention a new endeavor. You are truly appreciated.

To my family, my children and husband, thank you for being patient and encouraging me every step of the way. I love you and appreciate you.

ABOUT THE AUTHOR

Lori Ann Davis has a unique and passionate approach to love and relationships, and believes that everyone deserves and can have the relationship of their dreams. Her mission is to provide the skills you need in order to have the relationship you deserve.

She has a master's degree in psychology with over 30 years' experience empowering individuals and couples to live richer, happier lives. She provides relationship coaching to people throughout the world. Her practice spans the spectrum from dating and singles to working through divorce to renewing long-term marriages.

She is the author of *Unmasking Secrets to Unstoppable Relationships: How to Find, Keep, and Renew Love and Passion in Your Life*, *365 Ways to Ignite Her Love*, and *A Couples Love Journal*, and is a contributing author to *Ready, Set, Date*. She is also one of the coaches on the documentary show *Radical Dating*.

Visit her website at LoriAnnDavis.com

CPSIA information can be obtained
at www.ICGtesting.com
Printed in the USA
JSHW031340310720
7030JS00004B/12